Everything You Ever Wanted to Know About Bitcoin, But Were Too Afraid to Ask: All Your Questions Answered

By

Phillip J. Westbrook

"The reason why we have never found measure of wealth: we have never sought it."

--George S. Clayson, *The Richest Man in Babylon*

CONTENTS:

Everything You Ever Wanted to Know about Bitcoin,
But Were Too Afraid to Ask

INTRODUCTION

Many newcomers to the cryptocurrency world consider Bitcoin to be an impenetrable enigma. Talks by computer scientists of distributed ledgers, digital hashes, Ethereum, FinTech, hard forks, and nonces leave the casual observer overwhelmed and unnecessarily confused. This book is designed to help you tackle these cryptocurrency questions so that you're left with not only an understanding of the cryptocurrency world, but also a deep appreciation of its concepts and how it works (hint: it works in the same way money does). This book will be filled with plenty of illustrations to help you understand the concepts not only in writing, but visually as well. In addition, we will explore topics such as Bitcoin mining, transactions, and security. A large component of this work—and Bitcoin in general—is how it relates to money and how it is fundamentally different from currency, as we know it.

Bitcoin may initially seem quite confusing, but similar to many concepts, once basic definitions are defined and we delve into its basic concepts, you will be much more knowledgeable about cryptocurrency.

While many 'crypto' concepts draw the (often unwanted) attention of futurists and science-savvy dilettantes, there exist many practical applications to cryptocurrency that have the potential to revolutionize various aspects of our day to day lives, including: banking, personal and financial investments, and even mortgages and home loans.

Still others with a more dollar-conscious mind may view Bitcoins—or other competing cryptocurrencies—as a potential money making machine. At the time of this writing, the value of Bitcoin has absolutely skyrocketed from being worth less than a dollar two years ago, to exceeding $10,000 per Bitcoin. This means that if you invested $1,000 in Bitcoin in 2014, you'd be a millionaire many times over by the time of this writing.

This book is designed to help the average reader learn more about Bitcoin, but will also be useful for those seeking to understand the theoretical and financial underpinnings of Bitcoin as a powerful investment tool.

How is Bitcoin Money?

Before we delve into the intricacies of Bitcoin, it is first necessary to show where this 'money' is ensconced in—cryptocurrency. This term seems to scare a lot of people (unnecessarily) because it seems foreign to our physical world of euros, dollars, yuan, and rupees. The word *crypto* stems from the Greek word 'kriptos' meaning hidden or secret. However, there is nothing secret about this hidden currency of Bitcoin (we all know about it after all).

The only difference between any cryptocurrency and paper money is that while we can touch and see paper money, cryptocurrencies are 'invisible' so to speak—they only exist online.

Initially, this seems quite scary, no? If I have a million euros in the bank, but can't see it or hold it, is it really there? Perhaps even more important, will anyone believe that I have money there? Will it be worth anything, or will it simply be considered Monopoly money? In order to answer this question, we must develop a more nuanced understanding of money and how it influences the cryptocurrency world.

So what is money? For some, it is the root of all evil. For others, such as George Bernard Shaw, *lack of* money is the root of all evil. While Shaw may be more poetically inspired, he captures an essential point—money itself is just a tool by which we sell and purchase goods. Let's take a look at the trajectory of money over the past few millennia to understand where it is going. The answers to these questions will take us through an adventure beginning in ancient history, medieval China, through credit cards, and finish with Bitcoin.

A Brief History of Money:

If we look back at the last section, we saw that money is simply a *tool* by which we conduct transactions—but this was not always the case. For millennia, our ancestors did not trade using money, but rather through a system called **barter**.

BARTER:

Let's imagine that in the village of Bedrock, Fred and Wilma Flintstone are seeking to sell some of their wool to their neighbor. Since there are no euros or marks, the only option they have is to sell their wool in return for another product, say wheat. These are the basics of the barter system—one group needs material for clothing and another needs food, so they trade their products at whatever value they consider adequate.

Astute observers may already see a problem developing here—how much wool is wheat worth? It's a bit difficult to tell, so humanity essentially eyeballed these sorts of transactions for thousands of years. Clearly, this is not the most precise of transaction systems, but at the time, it worked quite nicely. Money developed from this system because in a world where people are consistently trying to cheat each other and gain a slight edge over their neighbors,[1] a more precise unit of measurement is required.

---

[1] It should be noted that while the modern man would immediately consider the option of extracting every bit of wool from one's neighbor for the least amount of wheat, it did not seem to occur that much to our ancestors. As proof of this, the barter system lasted for millennia. If there were extreme problems with people cheating the system to benefit themselves, this system of exchanging goods would not have lasted too long. Perhaps societal and familial pressures from others gave an impetus for people to treat each other more fairly in their transactions.

Fred and Wilma can trade with their neighbors in their village openly and conscientiously because if they try to cheat their neighbors, their community will shun them. However, eventually people began trading with others in different communities. The Silk Route, for example, traversed dozens of countries and two continents, connecting Europe to China. We cannot expect people to act nobly when they are conducting transactions with others in a foreign land and in different languages.

GOLD:

So eventually, they developed a system where they can trade a valuable object, like a gem or gold, for their product. Now we see the development of money. In leaving the world of wool and wheat, now we enter the world of gems and gold, where they may be traded in lieu of the other products. On one hand this makes sense, gold doesn't rot, spoil, it is resilient, it's quite compact, and can be used for pretty much any transaction. However, the same problem persists: how much gold is a kilo of wheat worth? There is no objective answer to this, and if every answer is subjective, then nobody's winning. Additionally, how can someone know that the gold used in a trade is legitimate? The answer came from governments.

COINS

When people began congregating into larger and larger groups, they formed tribes, chiefdoms, and kingdoms. In such large communities, it became impossible to discern between real gold and counterfeits. So the chiefs, kings, pharaohs, and emperors decided to 'mark' the gold coins with their stamp of accreditation. Gold slowly became more the metal of choice because of its permanence and malleability—it could easily be engraved with the king's seal. Now that coins were authenticated with the full backing of the local government, the king was essentially ensuring their credibility. For the next millennia, and even today, coins were the preferred method of conducting transactions. However, something interesting happened in China during the 13th and 14th centuries.

PAPER CURRENCY:

Chinese merchants soon grew tired of carrying tons of heavy copper coins in their boats. These coins were so cumbersome that they not only weighed their boats down, they prevented merchants from loading their boats with more of their products.

Furthermore, should anything happen to the ship, these copper coins sunk to the bottom of the ocean, never to be recovered. To solve this problem, they developed a clever solution. Merchants in Peking, Shanghai, and Guangzhou collectively decided that they would carry pieces of marked paper[2] to represent copper coins.

When they docked in the mainland, these pieces of marked paper—also known as 'flying money' because a strong wind could send a ship's paper flying—could be traded for coins. Eventually, this system of using paper to represent more valuable products caught on, and two centuries later, the local dynastic governments began printing their names and bestowing their stamps of approval on the paper, rendering it paper currency.

---

[2] At that time, China was known for pioneering a rudimentary form of paper from papyrus. Since they had papyrus to spare, paper money became the rule of the sea for Chinese merchants.

TODAY:

Paper currency clearly exists to this day in the form of British pounds, dollars, rials, and pesos. The principles also remain the same. The only difference between dollars and Monopoly money is the government's stamp of approval upon the dollar bill, thereby ensuring that every subject agrees that one dollar is worth exactly that, and cannot be traded for a bill of a different value. The same concept applies to Bitcoin, and every other currency. Euros and rubles are only worth their value *because* we all agree upon it.

The moment people begin thinking that yen and rupees aren't worth anything, we'll see their values drop. As we will later explore, **Bitcoin works under the same rules**. Before we jump from paper money to Bitcoin however, we have to pass through another revolutionary new idea in the history of money: credit cards. Much of Bitcoin's success has to do with the relationship between credit cards and banks, so it is important to check out how credit cards have influenced our daily lives in the 21st century

CREDIT CARDS:

When most people think of credit cards, they likely imagine American Express, MasterCard, Visa, and Discover. While all of these cards are surely considered credit cards, did you know that the precursor to these cards originated in medieval Europe? In a largely illiterate and uneducated society where most individuals could only perform basic math, a unique and clever method of keeping track of payments emerged in the form of tally sticks.

TALLY STICKS:

The concept is relatively simple: carve a few notches on a stick and split the stick in two. Let's imagine that in a Swiss canton, Mr. Cartier owes twenty francs to Mr. Baume. In order to show both parties that one owes money to another, they agree to carve twenty notches onto a tally stick. This tally stick is then cut (along the notches) so that each person has twenty half-notches on their stick. Once Mr. Cartier pays his creditor the twenty francs, the two of them put the sticks together, align up the notches, and complete the transaction.

Tally sticks additionally have a built-in counterfeiting measure. We must remember that this was a time before power tools and these sticks were broken by hand, meaning that the jagged edges of the wood would have to line up perfectly between creditor and debtor, rendering it difficult to fake a transaction or scratch off a notch. To help you understand what how tally sticks work, *Figure 1* below illustrates this rather ingenious concept.

Figure 1: Tally Sticks[3]

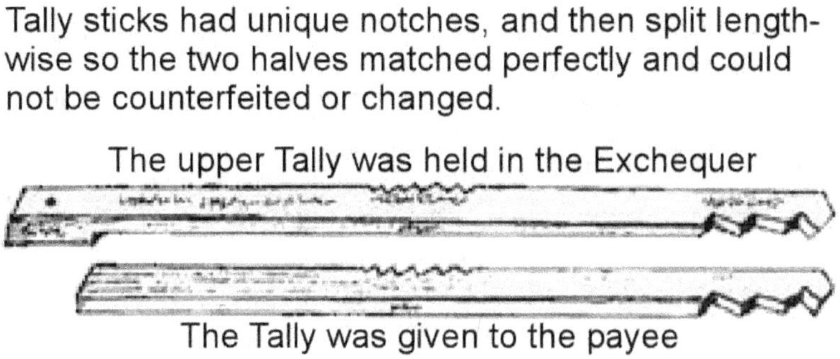

Tally sticks had unique notches, and then split length-wise so the two halves matched perfectly and could not be counterfeited or changed.

The upper Tally was held in the Exchequer

The Tally was given to the payee

This method of payment existed in Medieval Europe for centuries and it was not abolished until 1826 in England. Not long after the abolition of tally sticks[4] did credit cards become 'the name of the game' for many consumers.

E-COMMERCE:

---

[3] Photo taken from The Ben Williams Library, found at http://benwilliamslibrary.com/blog/wp-content/uploads/2015/04/th.jpg

[4] The British even used them for taxation purposes before they were abolished!

Unlike tally sticks, credit cards skyrocketed the transaction world into cyberspace, with most transactions occurring between credit cards and businesses. Also differing from tally sticks is that credit cards can charge interest—a concept that was eschewed and considered usury under canon law during the Middle Ages in Europe.

SUMMARY:

Something interesting is happening here, no? Let's briefly recount this 'ascent of money'[5] from the beginning of time to the present:

- At one time money didn't exist, as the general system of trading was barter.

---

[5] I credit this term to Niall Ferguson, who named his *magnum opus* 'The Ascent of Money.'

- Then money went from being the product itself to becoming precious gemstones and gold.

- Over time, gold became the preferred method of transactions, mostly because leaders could engrave their names and profiles onto the gold coins. While this was revolutionary enough, the gold itself still had a (largely symbolic) value. Gold itself cannot clothe or feed a person, but it's what it can buy that matters. As evidence of this, for example, *the Inca people could not comprehend how the Spanish were willing to kill every last one of them to extract what they considered to be a relatively useless yellow metal in the ground.*

- The transition to gold was impressive, but when that became cumbersome, the Chinese developed paper money, which rules to this day.

- Meanwhile in Europe, tally sticks allow people to borrow and loan money accurately, becoming the precursor to credit cards.

- Money has transferred from gems, to gold, to paper, to cards, to now with Bitcoin, disappearing altogether.

How Does Bitcoin Play Into this Trajectory in the World of Money?

So how does Bitcoin fit into the monetary world?

What exactly is so different about cryptocurrencies that alters the trajectory of money itself?

Well as we can see throughout the history of money, the value of money has become more and more subjective. Fred Flintstone knew exactly how much food he needed for the day, and was able to trade his wool for the day's wheat. Yet gold, although valuable enough, cannot be eaten. It needs to be traded for food.

The same logic holds for paper money; its worthless in and of itself and quite cheap to produce. For example, the US Mint spends more or less the same amount on the production of a five-dollar bill than a one hundred-dollar bill. The important thing to note is that the Mint *spends* money on *producing* money.

This aspect is quite counterintuitive to the currency world. This is also partially why gold went out of fashion—it had to be mined. During the Great Recession years, an interesting concept emerged from the shadows of plummeting stocks—what if we can create a currency that was free to produce and could only be generated through work? Here is where Bitcoin jumps into the currency world.

A Brief History of Bitcoin:

SHADOWY BEGINNINGS:

In 2008, an anonymous computer scientist by the name of Satoshi Nakamoto developed what we now call Bitcoin. Legends, rumors, and conspiracy theories abound about who exactly is Satoshi Nakamoto. Truth is, we have little to go on when it comes to Satoshi—and this may be a pseudonym for another person or group of people. Judging from the name, one would initially be led to believe that this person is a Japanese man. However, there have several audio clips with this individual and all accounts indicate an American man, without the slightest hint of a Japanese accent.

While evidence such as this lends itself to irregularities and suspicions regarding the true nature of Satoshi, others have hypothesized that Satoshi Nakamoto is a *nom de guerre* for a group of computer scientists and that Bitcoin is a more collective endeavor rather than the brainchild of any single individual.

These rumors may be the most off-putting aspect of Bitcoin for future investors, buyers, and consumers. If we don't know who is really behind Bitcoin, and if they have gone to these lengths to hide themselves, do they have sinister motives? People continue to speculate about these questions and there still don't seem to be any decisive answers. However, let's leave the world of cloaks and daggers and enter cyberspace. Rumors and speculation aside, Bitcoin solves many problems that currently exist with currency.

How is Bitcoin Different than paper currency?

THE INTERNET NECESSITY:

Unlike paper currency, Bitcoin operates solely in the world of computers, and in order to access Bitcoin, you must have Internet. As many reading this book can already surmise, right off the bat, Bitcoin helps one group over another. Predictably, new advances also benefit the richer 'Global North' over the generally poorer 'Global South.' Helene in Denmark may have easy access to Internet in Copenhagen. She may be able to walk from her home to any café and never lose Internet connection. Unfortunately, Daoud in Djibouti may have a tougher time gaining access to Internet, which may only be found in the town center and be prohibitively expensive.

It is true that Bitcoin is free to create (gold has to be mined and paper money must be printed), but if Bitcoin has any cost, it is the unrecovered cost of an Internet connection. Clearly the main difference between Bitcoin and any other physical currency is that while Internet connection does cost money, it can be used for almost anything and not just conducting financial transactions.

We have purposefully informed you of Bitcoin's main drawbacks first, so that we can end this introduction on a positive note.

UNIVERSAL ACCEPTANCE:

Unlike physical currency that is limited to the national level (e.g., Canadian dollars are only valid in Canada, and not in New Zealand), one of the main benefits of Bitcoin is that, since it's an Internet-based currency, it is universally accepted.

Essentially, if Sandra in Spain wants to send some money to her friend, Alex, in Australia, she can do so with Bitcoin cognizant that this cryptocurrency is equally valid in Madrid as it is in Melbourne. In this sense, Bitcoin is the first truly international and universal currency[6] that transcends borders, cultures, and languages.

While the euro may come in second, no physical currency can compete with Bitcoin's universality. Again, its transcendence of borders is valid, but this only exists if the user has access to Internet. Because of this, access to Bitcoin is more limited in what scholars call 'developing countries.'

---

[6] This statement, of course, must be footnoted with some talk of other attempted-international currencies. During the years of Pan-Arabism, some Middle East states decided to join together to form one state—notably Syria, Iraq, and Egypt—meaning that they would have shared a currency. Similarly, and more importantly, the Euro has been adopted by dozens of states in Europe. The difference between these cases and Bitcoin is that the latter is completely transnational in that it is not bounded by geography, culture, or foreign boundaries.

INFLATION PROTECTION:

Ironically enough, the people that Bitcoin is poised to help most are those who are least likely to benefit from this new currency. Let me explain. Bitcoin is not subject to the same inflationary tendencies that physical currencies are susceptible to.

For those economically minded readers, **inflation** occurs when a country attempts to improve the living conditions of its subjects by printing money. These practices do not, in reality, improve anyone's living conditions; in fact, they make them worse. Because producers know that everyone has more money in their pockets, they feel comfortable charging more for their products.

The United States, for example, has experienced a constant (and controlled) inflation of 3% over the past thirty years. It is because of this that we hear of a full meal costing 50 cents back in the 1970s.

Inflation may not be much of a problem in a developed country like the United States, but it's more problematic in a place like Zimbabwe, which reached a record 79 billion percent in 2008! This means that if someone had 79 billion Zimbabwean dollars in 2016, it would be worth one Zimbabwean dollar today. How can anyone ever save money in these types of situations?

Well, Bitcoin may offer an answer: If private citizens in Zimbabwe decide to invest their money in Bitcoin and conduct transactions using this cryptocurrency, then they would be able to **hedge** (to use the financial term) against the Zimbabwean dollar.[7] The only way for Zimbabweans to conduct transactions using Bitcoin, however, is for them to have access to Internet. That said, even though many in developing countries have trouble accessing Internet, this technology is spreading to more and more people each day.

---

[7] In reality, many fiscally minded citizens of the developing world save their money in US dollars, British pounds, or euros, knowing that these currencies are more stable and less susceptible to inflationary practices in their home countries. This has become such a common practice that in countries like Venezuela, where the bolivar is decreasing in value every day, many citizens are refusing to conduct business in the local currency, preferring dollars instead.

Bitcoin has the potential to undermine all of the physical currencies that we have touched upon. Furthermore, the banking and credit card industries can greatly benefit from Bitcoin's peer to peer (P2P) transactions. All of these topics will be discussed in great detail in the next few chapters. First however, it is necessary to go through some technical terms relating to Bitcoin, cryptocurrencies, and blockchain technology. If you are already somewhat familiar with Bitcoin, feel free to skip this chapter, otherwise read on.

CHAPTER 2: CRYPTOCURRENCY LINGO

Computer scientists and cryptocurrency fanatics love to speak in complex technical terms that not only ensure that an esoteric audience is listening, it also makes them seem smart. Because of this, many people are afraid to delve deeper into Bitcoin. This chapter is designed to help you navigate through the oftentimes-confusing language surrounding Bitcoin.

In addition, we are including a glossary of very-much needed terms so that if the reader forgets any of these concepts, they can easily find them at the end of this work. First and foremost, as we have already noticed, cryptocurrencies are money that exists only online. The most famous of these currencies, of course, is Bitcoin. But how does Bitcoin work? The answer lies is blockchain technology.

THE BLOCKCHAIN:

This technology holds the core of Bitcoin's success together, so it's important to dive deeper into this meaning. However, the concept of the blockchain is rather complex and can be a bit cumbersome to explain. If you are merely looking to invest in Bitcoin, rest assured that you do not need to know every last detail of this chapter.

This section is mostly for those who are interested in understanding the foundational computer science principles in the bedrock of Bitcoin. For the casual investor and learner, very little of this comes into play and you will unlikely ever hear of this part of Bitcoin.

That said, it is still beneficial to have an understanding of how Bitcoin, by adopting blockchain technology, works. Understanding the blockchain will also give you a leg up on other Crypto novices and help you to make better financial decisions when it comes to investing and trading Bitcoin.

Blockchain technology, as the name suggests, is composed of both blocks and chains of data. But what does this mean? Surely it doesn't mean physical blocks and chains? Naturally, in cyberspace, blockchain technology refers to the system used by Bitcoin to conduct transactions. While there are blocks and chains in the computer, they are not physical. An illustration is in order. Below in *Figure 2* you will find an example of a computer blockchain separated into the components of each block and chain.

Figure 2: Blockchain Technology (Source: NextSpace)[8]

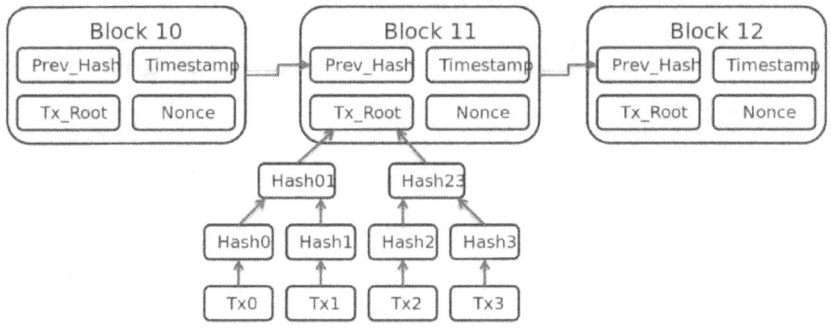

---

[8]   This   image   can   be   found   at
https://thenextspace.co/education/technology/blockchain-bitcoin-cryptotoken-masterclass/

The diagram in *Figure 2* illustrates a traditional blockchain. As you can see, each block is composed of four different components: a previous hash, a root hash (shown in the image as **Tx_root**, and also known as '**Merkle Root**' and '**Merkle Hash**'), a **timestamp**, and a **nonce**. Before we examine and define each of these terms, let's first examine the linkages between these blocks.

As most have predicted, they are called chains, connecting one block to its neighbor. Each chain connects one block to another, meaning that if you trace one blockchain all the way back, you'll find the first block in the chain. The chains are easy to explain, but now let's look into each block and see what they're all made up of.

BLOCKS:

Each block is made up of two different hashes: a previous hash and a root hash. But what in the world is a 'hash?' To many, hash is slang for a type of drug. Not so for Satoshi Nakamoto.

HASHES:

Hashes are bits of encrypted code 20 digits long (I.E., 0F23J3NOGB7WM314YWJD). These 20-digit hashes are difficult to reproduce and counterfeit because of the nearly infinite number of combinations available for each encrypted code. So let's look at each hash. First is the **previous hash**, which is probably the most complicated of all of the components (but really not too complicated).

The **previous hash** in *Figure 2* is a piece of code depicting where the block came from. This encrypted code not only informs us of the block's history by consisting of parts of the previous block. These components of its predecessor are depicted in *Figure 2* as Hash01 and Hash23. Meanwhile, each of these hashes are composed of two other hashes, Hash0 and Hash1, combine to form Hash01, and Hash2 and Hash3 compose Hash23. Each of these hashes also have their own previous hashes, and so on *ad infinitum*.

What's the Point of the Hashes?

Because of these previous hashes, we can know where each block has been. Imagine if Jenny has a $10 bill. She may know that she received this particular $10 as change for her shopping in Chicago. However, before this 10-dollar bill was in the cash register, Jenny has no idea where it was. It could have belonged to her neighbor, a wealthy billionaire, a counterfeiter, or a criminal.

With blockchain technology's previous hash, she could know exactly which account her money has passed through. Whereas in the physical world, we are only separated by one transaction, in blockchain, we can trace back the origins of each block (and therefore, Bitcoin) to its creation with the previous hash. Let's suppose that someone was bent on doing exactly this. They could trace previous hash to previous hash for a long time, or they could skip all of that and go directly to the **root hash**.

The **root hash**, or Merkle root/hash, shows the origins of any specific block and also serves a sort of ID card for the block. With this identification, the user can know that the block was created. Once a block is created, it cannot disappear. This creates an extra level of security because it doesn't necessarily allow Bitcoins to be laundered in the same way a drug trafficker can launder dollar bills. The root hash depicts the creation of the block and the previous hash shows where that block has been. What drug criminal would conduct transactions using these conditions?

The truth is very few because even though Pablo Escobar may want the big bucks, (aka Bitcoin), the blockchain technology ensures that there is always a paper trail. (This is also why drug dealers always deal in cash and never accept credit cards or checks for their illicit activities, but let's not digress). Back in the (legal) Bitcoin world, root hashes serve a necessary security function, but there are two more parts to each block.

TIMESTAMP:

The **timestamp** is probably the easiest part of the block to comprehend.

It simply shows when a new block was created. Not only does this timestamp authenticate the existence of the block, it also *cannot be altered in any way*. Furthermore, because the timestamp cannot be removed, there is an extra level of security built into the block within its existence in cyberspace. The timestamp allows anybody in the network to track the existence of any single block, making it effectively impossible to not leave a paper trail.

NONCE:

The final component of the block is the **nonce**. As a side note, many user accounts, Bitcoin aficionados, blockchain enthusiasts, and cryptocurrency buffs love to incorporate the word 'nonce' into their usernames, blogs, and even vernacular. Even though the name sounds weird, don't be alarmed; the concept is quite simple.

The nonce is simply a randomly generated number. When a human thinks of a randomly generated number, they may come up with 7 or 14. However, these numbers are easy to predict (and replicate). On the other hand, the nonces in blockchain technology are digits as high as 2^{31}, meaning that it is nearly impossible for a human to replicate this number.

The nonce, combined with the timestamp, root hash, and previous hash (which is itself composed of all the previous blocks), makes blockchain technology quite difficult to compromise, even with a super computer. However, there is one final aspect of blockchain technology, which is adopted by Bitcoin, which adds an almost impenetrable layer of security— the **distributed ledger**.

THE DISTRIBUTED LEDGER:

Another useful term to understand the basics of Bitcoin is the concept of a distributed ledger. Before we delve into what a *distributed ledger* is, we must first understand what a ledger is. Any reader familiar with accounting knows that the accountant keeps track of all financial documentation and transactions in what is called a **ledger**.

This **ledger** is a method of book-keeping at the heart of economic transactions, but more specifically, an accountant's ledger is a **centralized ledger**, because all of the information is stored in one location.

Let's imagine that Mr. Contador in Seville is the accountant for a small business. The firm needs to buy supplies and sell finished products just like any store. Mr. Contador's ledger would show incoming revenues along with expenses. Hopefully, if the business is doing well there will be more revenue that expenses, but the only way for Mr. Contador to know that is to track all of the transactions for the fiscal year. This is an example of a ledger, but more specifically, it's a **centralized ledger**.

All of the economic transactions are accounted for in one place, specifically Mr. Contador's ledger. Over the past few decades, modern-day companies have expanded this notion of the centralized ledger to not only include supercomputers, but also to conduct a whole host of transactions, ranging from email and calendar invites, to the traditional fiscal dealings.

For many years, centralized ledgers worked very well, as they contain accounts for recording transactions in one, safe location. However, over time, computer hackers realized that if they wanted to breach the security system of a large corporation, they would simply have to hack into one computer. This is a difficult feat, to be sure, but still possible.

Take a look at the security breaches into Yahoo's email accounts over the past year, and you'll see the potential dangers of a centralized ledger. A security breach to these computers is akin to somebody breaking into Mr. Contador's small business and stealing his ledger. Yet when this happens to a large corporation containing, such as Yahoo, millions of email usernames, passwords, and otherwise private information is compromised.

As is typical with computers, a security breach is not just the theft of a single email or password; it is a large-scale, systemic threat to the system that compromises all accounts and passwords, not just one. In order to combat this potentially disastrous scenario, Bitcoin adopts the concept of a **distributed ledger**. It's perhaps easier to visually observe the difference between a **centralized**, **decentralized**, and **distributed ledger** in the figure below.

Figure 3: Different Types of Ledgers (Source: Grissom 2017)[9]

---

[9] *Figure   3   is   taken   from   Grissom's   blog   at* https://steemit.com/crypto/@jfgrissom/who-controls-crypto-currencies

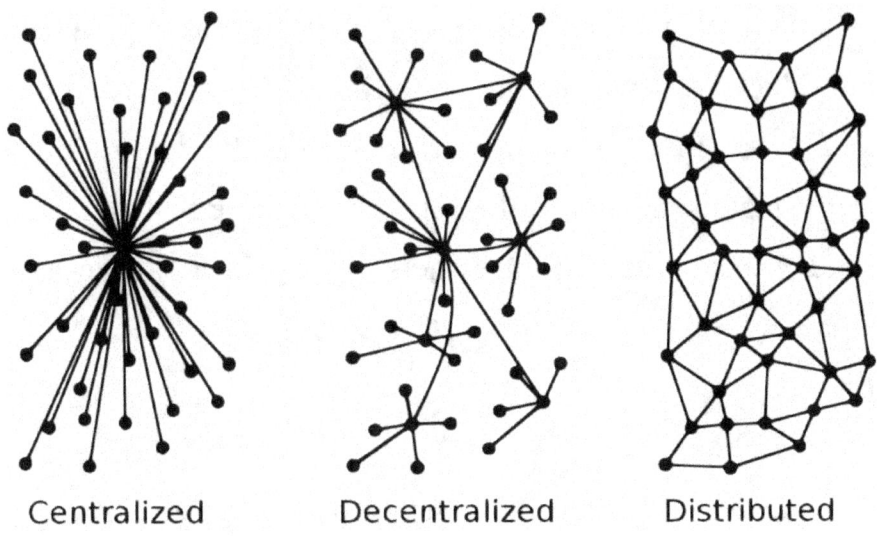

Centralized   Decentralized   Distributed

The centralized ledger works in the same way Mr. Contador's paper ledger worked. It held the information of all transactions in one centralized location (for Mr. Contador it was in his accounting book; for a multinational corporation it's in supercomputers).

A **decentralized ledger** conducts the same procedure on a smaller scale. This is considered somewhat safer than a centralized ledger because if a hacker attacks a supercomputer (shown as a node in the decentralized model), then only the accounts connected to that node get jeopardized. On the other hand, we see what a distributed ledger looks like in the right side of *Figure 3*.

In a **distributed ledger**, such as the one used by Bitcoin in its blockchain, when a file (called a block) gets saved, it does not only get saved onto the user's computer. It gets saved onto every single computer in the network. Suppose that Ahmad in Cairo wants to save a paper he's writing in a safe location online.

EXAMPLE:

- CENTRALIZED: If he saves his essay onto his laptop, this would be an example of a centralized ledger. If someone were interested in stealing Ahmad's paper, they would have to break into his laptop to retrieve the information.

- DISTRIBUTED: However, let's imagine that Ahmad thinks his paper has the potential to revolutionize his industry and wants to keep his information as safe as possible. He could choose to save his work onto a distributed ledger in a blockchain. This would encrypt the data so that only he can access it and then save his essay onto every single computer in the blockchain network.

This means that if someone were to hack the system, they would be forced to break into each computer in the network, which potentially could be millions of users, at the same time and alter the information identically across all of the computers.

While I hesitate to call a distributed ledger unbreakable, nothing is impossible. However, as far as security goes, distributed ledgers are by far more secure than centralized and decentralized ledgers.

Again, if you are the casual investor in Bitcoin, much of this information is not absolutely vital to your goals to your goals, and if it doesn't make much sense to you, don't sweat it. However, if you are interested in learning the intricacies of Bitcoin and investing more in cryptocurrencies in general, this may be useful information to know before you bet your money on Bitcoin. In learning these concepts you'll know "enough to be dangerous" as they say. And you'll be able to hold your own in any Bitcoin discussion.

Summary:

Let's quickly review what we have learned about Bitcoin:

THE BAD:

- First, the bad news: yes, Bitcoin's founder(s) is an anonymous person, and it is understood that this does not bode well for those looking to invest in this cryptocurrency as it is difficult to trust Satoshi Nakamoto, if that is indeed this person's name.

- It is additionally suggestive that if this anonymous person speaks with an American accent, why is his name Japanese? Legends and folk tales may lend credence to Bitcoin's mystique, but it provides little comfort for future investors that may be more interested in a profit and a secure investment.

- The next downside regarding Bitcoin is that it is only available to those with Internet. This drawback should not deter future investors—especially since access to Internet is growing exponentially—but it should be noted that the people who are best positioned to gain from Bitcoin are precisely those who cannot have access to it because Internet is either unavailable or else prohibitively expensive.

THE GOOD:

- Now that the bad news is out of the way, we can focus on how Bitcoin can be a force for progress in the investment and banking industry. We saw how the Zimbabwean person can now hedge against their currency by conducting transactions in Bitcoin and how it may be used to bet against inflation.

- Bitcoin is a cryptocurrency that works by using blockchain technology along a distributed ledger. As we saw, blockchain technology is composed of—as the name insinuates—blocks and chains. The chains are easy enough to understand, but the blocks are a bit more complex and are composed of the following: root hash, previous hash, timestamp, and nonce.

- All of these blocks and chains are then saved onto a distributed ledger, which records transactions onto every single computer in the network—a figure that can reach millions of users.

You now have the basic tools to understand the history and building blocks of Bitcoin. In the next section, we are going to examine the finer points of Bitcoin (e.g., security, mining, etc.), how it relates to our lives, and how it potentially revolutionizes banking and investment.

CHAPTER 3: YOUR BITCOIN QUESTIONS ANSWERED

In this section, we are going to tackle the most pressing questions revolving around Bitcoin and cryptocurrencies. Each question will be marked in **bold**, with the answer succeeding it. There may be many different types of readers here: potential investors, Bitcoin miners, cryptocurrency enthusiasts, casual learners, and possible users of Bitcoin. Because of the variety of readers, we are splitting up the questions into broad categories so that you can skip to the question that is most pertinent to you. The first question may interest the general public:

What is the obsession with Bitcoin?

Bitcoin has had an incredible trajectory over the past few years, skyrocketing from worth nearly nothing to over $10,000 in the second half of 2017. What started off as a sort of computer experiment has turned out to be a great success! But what happened here?

In the long term, there has been a general tendency to cross country frontiers in the world market. Large-scale advances, such as the trend of globalization and financialization that took the world by storm in the post-Cold War Era traversed many nation-state lines. People are much more comfortable in dealing with business negotiations in other countries than ever before! Because of this, the 'marketplace' was something that used to exist on the local level.

With the advent of the Internet, cross country jets, and computer technology, now the 'marketplace' exists worldwide. Bitcoin is just another component of this expansion and globalization. Keep in mind that in 2002, dozens of European states decided to forfeit their national currencies, be it the franc, the mark, the peso, or the lira, in favor of a collective currency—the euro. This was unprecedented! Fifty years ago, nobody would have thought that these countries, which had fought against each other in two world wars, would combine forces to create a united currency.

Yet here we are in 2017, not only with the euro, but also with Bitcoin—the world's first truly universal currency.

So why the obsession? Well Bitcoin is a revolutionary new idea, bedrocked on pre-existing notions. Remember how we spoke about how money has gone from gold, to paper, to cards, to disappearing altogether? Bitcoin is the embodiment of that last part of money. Because it cannot be physically held, its value is only what other people say it is. This may be fickle though because in the same way that the price of Bitcoin can skyrocket, it can just as easily plummet. Now that we have the bad news out of the way, let's move on to the good news.

IT'S A REVOLUTION:

Bitcoin can quite possibly revolutionize the banking and investment industry.

Picture this scenario:

Hans in Berlin owes his landlord his monthly rent that is due at the first of the month. His landlord, Gabrielle, is insistent that he pays his due on time.

However, Hans got paid from his job on the 30th and needs to take the money out of his bank account. It takes the bank three to five business days to process the money transfer from his job, and then takes a bit more for them to process Hans' withdrawal. Before you know it, a week passes, and Hans still has not paid Gabrielle. If this transaction were done with Bitcoin, Hans would have little trouble, as money can be passed from one person to another (called peer-to-peer transactions, or P2P) instantaneously. With Bitcoin, by adopting blockchain technology, when Hans gets paid, he can immediately transfer the money to Gabrielle without having to incur the penalties of paying his rent late.

This concept can be applied to almost any other industry. Imagine instantaneous investment banking or receiving money instantly from a friend instead of waiting the usual three to five business days.

In addition to the practical benefits to using Bitcoin in our daily lives, there exists a certain **mystique** regarding cryptocurrencies. Satoshi Nakamoto's enigmatic presence aside, Bitcoin seems to come at us from the future, and the stock market proves this. Before we delve into the concept of investing in Bitcoin (we will ask this question later), let's first see what problems Bitcoin solves. We have alluded to many of them throughout these sections, but there are tangible benefits regarding Bitcoin that we should explore.

What problems does Bitcoin solve?

FLAWS IN OUR CURRENT SYSTEM:

There exist a few problems with our current system of money. First of all, it costs money to make money. This in itself seems ludicrous. Take a look at these statistics: it costs the US Mint 4.9 cents to make a $1 bill and 10.9 cents to make a $5 bill. One would think that the price per unit would continue going up for larger bills due to the extra security measures that the Mint imprints onto every dollar, but this is not so! Amazingly enough, it costs the US Mint 10.3 cents to make a $10 bill and 10.5 cents to make $20 and $50 bills. Why the price of a $5 bill is more expensive than a $10, $20, or $50 bill is beyond the scope of this work (though perhaps economies of scale come into play here – but that is just speculation).

Naturally, given the large security measures, such as watermarks and magnetic strips, put in place into the $100 bill, a Benjamin costs 12.3 cents. The marginal gains from minting coins are almost not worth the hassle, with the cost of making one penny hovering at around 1.7 cents and nickels cost around 8 cents.[10] This means that the government actually loses money in order to produce money.

SAVING MONEY ON PRODUCING MONEY:

At one time, printing money was a way of ensuring that businesses and consumers could conduct transactions. With the end of the gold standard and the floating dollar, it has become less and less important to print money, as many transactions are already conducted online and without the physical transfer of cash.

---

[10] This information is largely taken from CNN Money, found here: http://money.cnn.com/2016/01/11/news/economy/u-s-coins/index.html

While you may not know it, most of your money already exists in cyberspace in the form of digital numbers on your telephone or computer screen. If banks, investment companies, Fortune 500 conglomerates, and small businesses began using Bitcoin as a standard currency, it would save governments (and therefore, taxpayers) the hassle of creating their own currencies.

OBLITERATING EXCHANGE RATES

Along this train of thought, have you ever passed by money exchange kiosks in the airport? Let's say Dimitrios in Athens travels to Johannesburg. He would have to exchange his euro for the South African Rand at the airport (and get ripped off with the exchange rates in the process). Bitcoin would effectively render this industry obsolete. Because it is universally accepted as a cryptocurrency, Bitcoin would work just as well in Greece as in South Africa.

However, just because that industry would be altered, doesn't mean that it will go away forever. Bitcoin is simply a strong competition for those physical currency exchanges. If they were smart, they would slowly adopt Bitcoin (and other cryptocurrencies) into their system of money exchange.

BENEFITTING THE MANY DESPITE CURRENCY SITUATIONS:

When a player like Bitcoin revolutionizes an industry, we must always ask ourselves, *cui bono*, who benefits? Well, if we were to answer honestly, it seems like those who invested in Bitcoin from the outset benefit most. That said, Bitcoin could always benefit more and more people, especially if the physical currencies around them are burning to the ground (e.g., the Zimbabwean dollar). However, we must also ask ourselves the opposite—who loses? Bitcoin has solved one problem, but may have created many enemies. If a cryptocurrency developed by an anonymous computer scientist can compete with the mighty dollar, euro, British pound, ruble, and yuan, then Bitcoin has managed to unite every single government against them. If there is any industry that governments hold a monopoly over, it's the currency making industry!

THE DESTRUCTION OF CURRENCY:

Up until Bitcoin, only governments have had the political fiat to print money for their constituencies. If Bitcoin undermines that power, then it has found something that all governments can agree upon. How nations will react to the ascent of Bitcoin still is in the speculative stage, but if Bitcoin poses a true threat to all fiat currencies, then the collective government response worldwide would be strong. While this scenario is unlikely, Bitcoin solves the problem that many travellers have had over the years; you lose money because you are exchanging money through a middleman. With Bitcoin, since you won't have to exchange money, there will be no middleman. Let's take a look at how else middlemen are sidelined with Bitcoin.

As we alluded previously, Bitcoin is also a valuable tool for speeding up P2P money exchanges. But that's not all. Because Bitcoin implements a distributed ledger to keep track of all money transfers, the system is much safer than if your friend gave you a $20 bill or if they electronically wired the same amount to your bank account.

Your encrypted information spread out over the entire network would be nearly impossible to jeopardize. Furthermore, precisely because Bitcoin is capable of conducting these P2P money transfers automatically, it does not need the fables (and hated) middleman.

WHAT BANKS ARE ACTUALLY DOING WITH YOUR MONEY:

The real reason why banks, investment institutions, and financial corporations take three to five business days to conduct even the simplest of transactions is because they have armies of accountants, clerks, and managers ensuring that the money goes from 'Point A' to 'Point B' correctly.

Also, and even moreso, it's because they're using your money for other banking functions and therefore they need to acquire the money back from somewhere to make a payment on your behalf. If you deposit money in your account, the bank will be using that money to lend to others and to fulfill loans while you may be under the delusion that your money is just sitting there.

Due to its distributed ledger, which effectively keeps an eye out over the entire system, Bitcoin transactions do not require this sort of manpower, and your money is readily available to you. If there is any problem that Bitcoin solves, it is that it automates currency exchanges. Bitcoin has effectively brought currencies into the 21st century by automating transactions that previously were laborious and costly.

Remember Hans and his landlord Gabrielle? The only reason it took Hans three to five business days to extract his money from the bank was because he had to wait for all of the middlemen in his bank to process his request. This not only takes time, it also costs the bank a lot of money because they have to pay all of these employees. It's no wonder that Fortune 500 companies are looking to **blockchain** technology (and by extension, Bitcoin) to streamline their accounting processes.

Bitcoin solves many important problems, and the ones listed above are just a few of them, but as we saw, it creates a few more. This begs the question, however, what is the point? Why should I use Bitcoin rather than fiat currency that works relatively well for my limited needs?

In the next section we are going to discover the ways in which you could use Bitcoin in your daily lives. You may realize that this is hardly different than how you would conduct day-to-day transactions using USD, Euros, Dinars and Rand.

How can we use Bitcoin?

INCREASING POPULARITY:

You may be surprised to find out that you can pay for online dating websites and the computer you're using to boot using Bitcoin! Due to its astronomic increase in popularity, Bitcoin is starting to be accepted by many corporations, online marketplaces, and even non-profits.[11] While it may not come as a surprise that companies, such as mint.com, which is a financial planning website, accepts Bitcoin, other companies, such as Microsoft, are getting in on the action.

Furthermore, you can donate to Save the Children or Wikipedia if you are so inclined, with Bitcoin. But the fun doesn't end there; Overstock has partnered with Coinbase to become the first major retailer to accept this cryptocurrency. Virgin Galactic and Peach Airlines have also thrown their hat into the ring. You can even use Bitcoin to buy a Tesla, and yes, OkCupid does accept Bitcoin.

Computer apps, such as Shopify and Square are also Bitcoin compatible. Finally, lest we get too anecdotal, you can even buy (some) food with Bitcoin, with Subway[12] and Magnificent Tea accepting this cryptocurrency.

---

[11]   The   following   information   is   taken   from https://steemit.com/bitcoin/@steemitguide/2017-top-list-of-big-companies-that-accept-bitcoin-and-cryptocurrencies

[12]   Subway's   stance   on   accepting   Bitcoin   can   be   found   at https://99bitcoins.com/who-accepts-bitcoins-payment-companies-stores-take-bitcoins/

Bitcoin has a long way to go before it can compete with the usability and ubiquity of the dollar, but the companies named above are not small or fringe corporations (well, Virgin Galactic comes close). Rather, they are respected and large corporations. More importantly, they are not just computer-based companies, but rather automotive (Tesla), encyclopedic (Wikipedia), restaurants and food (Subway), and consumer-based (Overstock).

What is most impressive is the sheer variety of all of these companies that have little to do with each other. Virgin Galactic and OkCupid have little in common other than the fact that they both accept payment through Bitcoin.

What is even more impressive is that the majority of the corporations named above have only recently begun accepting Bitcoin as payment. It seems like we are still in the growing phase of Bitcoin acceptance and that this trajectory has not plateaued over time. There are some exceptions. For example, Expedia, the online travel conglomerate, has accepted Bitcoin as payment since 2014. Similarly to Overstock, they are aligning themselves with Coinbase to accept this cryptocurrency.

Perhaps on a more worrying note, many computer hackers are hacking government databases, which, as you may have guessed, use centralized ledgers rather than the distributed ledgers of blockchain, and demand payment in Bitcoin! While these cases remain anecdotal, it is impressive that Bitcoin is considered a viable medium of exchange among criminals as well.

Why Doesn't Every Merchant Accept Bitcoin?

Yet, as always, we must ask ourselves why aren't more companies accepting Bitcoin as payment? Online investment information coming from the Motley Fool has a few suggestions. First, Bitcoin remains "exceptionally volatile, and even overnight settlements could result in businesses losing out on a lot of money."

They continue, stating that "Bitcoin prices plunged by more than $200 in a single day between June 25 and June 26. Businesses that had conducted transactions in Bitcoin with next-day settlement could have seen between 7% and 10% of their deal value depleted in a matter of hours (Williams 2017).[13] They have a point, but we will discuss investing in Bitcoin a bit later.

---

[13] Information taken from Sean William's article from July 6, 2017 found at https://www.fool.com/investing/2017/07/06/5-brand-name-businesses-that-currently-accept-bitc.aspx

The other reason why other companies are not investing in Bitcoin was already alluded to but needs a different slant: Bitcoin can become so popular that it may incur the ire of governmental regulators.

If Bitcoin begins "acting as a bridge currency for marijuana purchases looks like the perfect reason for U.S. lawmakers to consider imposing regulations on the cryptocurrency. As long as the government leaves bitcoin alone, it has an opportunity to thrive" (Ibid.). But let's be real—most governments may not allow Bitcoin to fully thrive without creating a system of checks and balances to hinder its progression.

The next question that we answer is quite possibly the most itching question that readers have, and accordingly, it will be the question with the longest response: how do we make money off Bitcoin? Because there are many ways to make money off Bitcoin, it is perhaps best to split up the question into two sections, which will be explained in greater detail below: mining and investing.

How do I make money off Bitcoin?

Isn't this the million-dollar (or Bitcoin, if you're so inclined) question? As mentioned in the previous section, there are two main ways to capitalize upon Bitcoin's success—**mining** and **investing**.

In keeping with the style of the book, let's start off with the more difficult topic of mining before we delve into the aspect of investing, which is admittedly more exciting. If you are interested in learning about the internal makings of Bitcoin, then this section ought to interest you, as it answers many mysteries surrounding Bitcoin. We know how fiat currency is made—it is minted at a government agency. However, how exactly are Bitcoin released into circulation?

BITCOIN MINING:

The method that most governments use to print paper money is much more cost effective than previous strategies. The Spanish, for example, nearly bankrupted themselves trying to find more and more gold in America. By those standards, the twelve cents it takes the US Mint to make a $100 Benjamin is quite efficient.

However, if we are to take currency (along with everything that comes with it) into the 21st century, then we would have to regenerate it for free. This is, more or less, how Bitcoin mining works. Clearly, when we are talking of **Bitcoin mining**, this does not refer to actual digging for gold—those days are long gone. In Bitcoin mining, users solve mathematical problems to gain more Bitcoin.

That last statement clearly deserves a more nuanced answer. Let's say that Venkat in Calcutta is interested in mining for Bitcoin. He can begin doing so by physically solving a math problem for Bitcoin. Usually, in the beginning, it's something simple, like 517 minus 314. As Venkat solves more and more math problems, they become more and more difficult. In return for Venkat's work solving math problems, he is rewarded with Bitcoins.

This essentially incentivizes him into solving more complex algorithms. However, soon Venkat is going to have a problem: there will come a time when he either cannot solve a math problem, or it will take too long for him to solve one. Essentially, the number of Bitcoin returned to Venkat for solving math problems (mining) is not worth the time he spent working on math problems.

So what can he do to solve this dilemma? He can subcontract friends to do the work for him, but that requires paying him off. If Venkat is astute, he'll create a computer program on his laptop to begin solving math problems at a faster rate than he can do so with pen and paper.

USING COMPUTERS:

Suppose that Venkat did this: he ditched his pen and paper and his computer began conducting math problems for him. In return for his computer's labor, Venkat received Bitcoin. In the early days of Bitcoin, this was quite a possibility. However, times have changed. Pretty soon, Venkat's computer processor could not cope with the volume of others also mining for Bitcoin by solving these algorithmic problems.

USING COMPUTER "STEROIDS"

Pretty soon, others discovered that if they insert computer graphic cards into their computers, they could mine for Bitcoin at a faster rate than simply using a computer processor. So Venkat goes to his local store and buys some of these graphic cards and inserts them into his computer to continue mining for Bitcoin. This works relatively well until his electric bill comes in.

It turns out that these graphic cards not only cost a fortune in and of themselves, they also require extreme amounts of electricity. This not only lowers the comparative advantage Venkat has over his peers, it also heats up his computer to dangerous levels.[14] To further complicate matters, now because of the increasing number of people worldwide mining for Bitcoin, Venkat's margins are getting slimmer and slimmer. Once upon a time, when very few people believed that Bitcoin could work, one could generate enough Bitcoin by solving problems by hand. Now, it's more difficult – and will get more complicated still!

As in everything in (capitalistic) life, if there is a demand, supply will follow, and that is exactly what happened with Bitcoin mining. Eventually, the process of mining became commercialized. Reprogrammed computer chips were developed and sold as alternatives to the (now) old gaming chips. Not only were these products much faster than their predecessors, they were exponentially faster than doing this work by hand. By today's standards these computer chips would be considered quite rudimentary solutions to mining for Bitcoin.

---

[14] I've heard of cases of people even putting their computers in freezers because they were getting so heated from computer applications.

Eventually, a much faster option developed: application-specific integrated circuit chips, generally abbreviated to ASIC. These circuit chips are much faster than their predecessors and require less electricity per math problem, meaning that Venkat's electric bill would not cost more than the Bitcoin that he earned and that he won't have to put his laptop in a freezer to keep it from burning up. ASIC chips are another truly revolutionary development in the field of Bitcoin, but there is yet one more option that Venkat has that could allow him to make more money off Bitcoin mining.

TEAMING UP:

In the nascent years of Bitcoin, many miners were what we'd consider loners—they liked their computer world eschewing most other opportunities. But let's imagine that Venkat is a sociable fellow and has many friends who are interested in Bitcoin mining. How could they collectively generate more Bitcoin than their peers?

What has been developed over time is the process of '**pool mining.**' Pool miners are essentially a group of friends that get together to mine for Bitcoin. By gathering into groups to solve complex math equations, economies of scale become more important.

Whereas in the past, Venkat could simply buy an ASIC card and use that to mine for Bitcoin, by combining with friends, they can mine for Bitcoin at a quicker rate than everyone else, giving them a competitive edge. By conducting math problems in unison, they can mine for more Bitcoin at a faster rate than before. There's an interesting point here though.

As we can see, even if Venkat were a genius, he would never have been able to compete with the astronomical increase in technology, beginning with gaming chips and continuing with ASIC chips. No human can conduct enough math problems quickly enough to compete with computers, and later on, pools of computers. But how do computers solve these problems, and why does it consume so much electricity and labor? The answer may surprise you.

When Venkat solves a math problem, he does his best to get the answer correct on the first try. In order to do this, he uses previous mathematical skills to add or subtract a number. The ASIC chips, along with their predecessors do not work in such an efficient manner. Rather than solving a complex algorithm by using the same mathematical principles that Venkat uses, Bitcoin mining software solves problems through what computer scientists call *brute force*.

Brute force is essentially a method of problem solving where the computer randomly guesses answers to a math problem. Once the correct answer is guessed, the machine moves on to the next problem. As you can tell this is very unlike Venkat's method of problem solving, and as you likely guess, this is also how his electric bill becomes so high. Brute force, because of the high volume of guesses that ASIC chips conduct, becomes very energy intensive.

But why does Bitcoin have miners solving math problems?

This seems like an unusual way to circulate a currency. It is understood that fiat currency must be printed in order to circulate it; gold and silver logically have to be mined. But what happens when a computer is mining for Bitcoin? Essentially, **these math problems that Bitcoin miners solve are transactions going on within the blockchain network**.

Let's imagine that Miguel in Mexico City wants to give $50 to his friend, Barbara in Buenos Aires. Since it's impractical to convert from one currency to another, Miguel decides to give her money through Bitcoin. When this request gets placed through the blockchain network, computers mining for Bitcoin answer the calling through **brute force**. Once a computer solves the problem, it gets passed on to the next math equation, and so on.

So in essence what Bitcoin miners are doing is approving transactions along the blockchain. Because these transactions are done through computers and not manually—which are how many banks still operate—Bitcoin's transactions get solved 'immediately.' So Miguel's money reaches Barbara very quickly and much more efficiently than a single bank transaction would take.

MINING OFFERS YET ANOTHER LAYER OF SECURITY:

Mining in Bitcoin world offers a *proof of work*. Essentially, now the Bitcoin miners approved of Miguel's transfer to Barbara, he cannot double spend that money anywhere else.

In the same way he couldn't use those $50 at the grocery store and give them to Barbara, he cannot 'double dip' in the Bitcoin blockchain. If he were to try to do so, Miguel would have to out-compute all other miners in the network—a feat that is practically impossible.

This lends itself to a degree of security within the blockchain, as nobody can simply 'create' money out of nowhere. It also makes it more difficult to counterfeit the cryptocurrency. While counterfeiting dollars may be difficult enough because of the levels of security built into each unit, if there is such a way to counterfeit Bitcoin, it is unknown to me. There are simply too many eyes over the network. Also unlike fiat currency, an unknowing store clerk may inadvertently accept a fake bill without know it. This cannot be said for Bitcoin because every miner would know of any counterfeit charges or transactions.

MINERS = THE HUMAN CHECKS AND BALANCES OF CRYPTOCURRENCY

Because of this, miners act as the Mint in fiat currency. They stamp their seals on each dollar and euro, ensuring the currency's authenticity. These Bitcoin miners are essentially notaries—but ensuring the validity of each transaction, they are keeping an eye over the entire blockchain.

Miners' jobs therefore, are very important, and as a reward for their labor, they are compensated in Bitcoin. This not only allows mining to be profitable; it also gives them an incentive to keep on mining. And here is the unique aspect of Bitcoin, the more miners there are on the blockchain, the more secure the network is, because miners keep an eye out over all Bitcoin transactions.

How Many Bitcoins Are There, and Will They Ever Stop Circulating Them?

Now that we have mentioned Bitcoin transactions, here's an important note regarding the number of Bitcoin in circulation: Remember how we mentioned that Bitcoin could be used to hedge against imprudent printing of fiat currency (the Zimbabwean dollar for example, with its 79 billion percent inflation rate)? Satoshi Nakamoto kept this in mind and limited the circulation to be 21 million Bitcoins. These Bitcoins would be released every ten minutes, which was initially how long it would take for the blockchain to reload.

Currently, it's much quicker due to the increase and popularity of mining. Originally however, there was a block reward for mining Bitcoin, which was a maximum of 50 per hour. Because of the ten-minute lag, a miner could only create six blocks per hour, which equates to 210,000 blocks in a year (assuming no breaks for the computer, of course). Additionally, every four years, the number of blocks created by mining will half.

For example, currently, the supply growth is held stagnant at 12.5 Bitcoins for every ten minutes. In four years, this number won't be at 12.5, but rather half of that—6.25 Bitcoins per ten minutes. Four years later, this number would also half: 3.125 Bitcoins per ten minutes, and so on, up until the magic number of 21 million Bitcoins is reached. It is predicted that the 21 million count will be reached between 2040 and 2050. For that math whiz reader out there who is interested in figuring out how all these numbers are related, here is the formula: $210{,}000 \times 50 \, [(1 / (1 - 0.5)] = 21$ million Bitcoin.

But what happens once 21 million Bitcoin is reached?

This is an interesting question. There are currently over 7 billion people in the world, and if Bitcoin's aim were to be a universal currency, then on average, every person would have 0.003 Bitcoins. Pretty pathetic, huh? Well, Satoshi has a secret. Once the magic number of 21 million is reached, the value of every Bitcoin will simultaneously be cut in half. Don't freak out though!

This does not mean that you will be left with half of the amount of money you had before. Far from it. The reason for the halving is to accommodate more and more users. The value of Bitcoin will eventually be determined not by the number of this cryptocurrency in circulation, but by the laws of supply and demand.

This means that it doesn't matter how many Bitcoin you actually have. What's important is how many you have in comparison to other users in the Bitcoin blockchain. This, in the end, is the true value of money. For better or worse, money is what some people have and others do not.

George Bernard Shaw's statement, quoted in the introduction, is still true: *lack of* money is the root of all evil. Now that we have a rudimentary understanding of how Bitcoin works, let's look at the more interesting aspect of this cryptocurrency—how to invest in it.

How Do I Invest In Bitcoin?

If the previous section on Bitcoin mining left you a bit confused, don't worry at all. There is another, more efficient manner of making money off Bitcoin: investing.

Now clearly this comes with some caveats. There is the possibility that when investing in any endeavor, the individual may lose all or some of their money, and Bitcoin is no different. There is something to be said for not putting all of your eggs in one basket, and Bitcoin has the potential to be an exploding basket.

For professional advice on investing in Bitcoin, it is suggested that you speak to your financial advisor. On a less professional note, here is some information on how Bitcoin has risen from being worth nothing to rising over $10,000 per Bitcoin at the end of 2017!

Figure 4: Value of Bitcoin (Source: Bitcoin.com)[15]

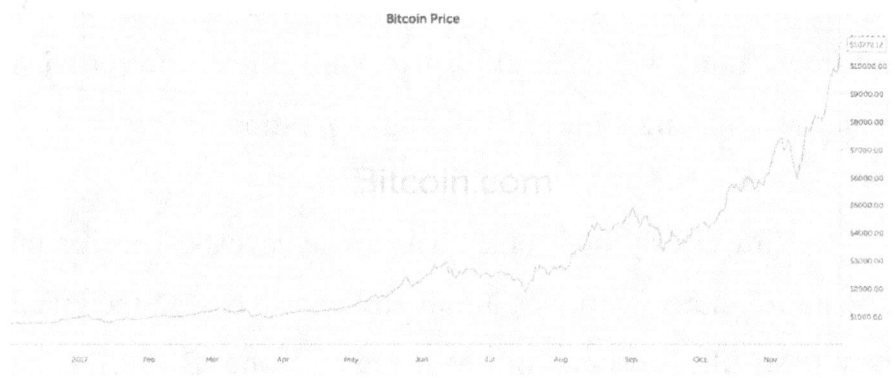

Check out the value of Bitcoin over the past year. Keep in mind that this chart only shows 2017. *Figure 4* only shows the trajectory of Bitcoin in 2017, but you get the idea. It was worth practically nothing in 2012 and now ranges in the $10,000 area.

---

[15] Information taken from https://charts.bitcoin.com/chart/price

Before we get too ahead of ourselves, let's remember that there are two dependent variables working against each other in this chart. First, obviously is the value of Bitcoin against the dollar. Second, and perhaps more hidden, is the changing value of the dollar.

However, unlike Bitcoin's meteoric rise, the dollar has been slightly increasing in value against other currencies over the past few years. Clearly, it's Bitcoin's value that has greatly increased and not insane dollar inflation. At the risk of getting rid of this rosy picture, let's look at another graph illustrating the rise of Bitcoin from 2011 to this September.

Figure 5: Rise of Bitcoin 2011-2017 (Source: CoinDesk 2017)[16]

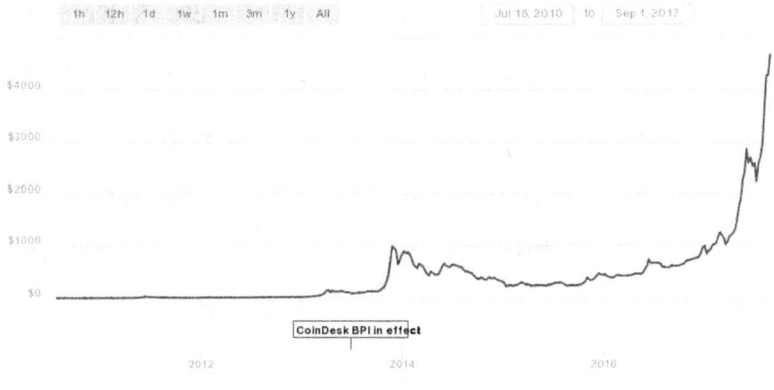

---

[16] This graph was taken from https://www.coindesk.com/price/

In this graph, we generally see the rise of Bitcoin, especially in 2017. However, let's take a look at what happened in 2014. We observe a strong increase in value from being worth absolutely nothing to $1000 in a matter of a few months. Then, almost immediately, we see the price drop precipitously.

This is known as a financial or economic bubble, similar to the ones that we saw in the housing market before the 2008 and the dot-com boom in the 1990s. A **bubble** occurs when the trading of a specific asset strongly exceeds the real value of those assets.

For example, during the recent housing crisis that affected most of the United States, homes were selling for double or triple of what their actual prices were. So if a home that originally cost $200,000 was sold in 2007, someone would have likely bought it for half a million dollars. But, no matter, people simply kept on buying! And if that happens, property owners are simply going to charge even higher prices.

Eventually some investors realized that the housing market could no longer support such ballooning price tags for single-family dwellings, and the values of homes came crashing down (and the stock market with it). The values of these homes perhaps dropped to less than what it cost to build them. So what happened to the family that bought a home for half a million dollars? They are paying off a home at a mortgage for a home worth $500,000 when, in reality, their home is only worth $200,000.

When situations like these occur, the 'bubble' bursts. Here's the tricky part: we never really know *beforehand* when the bubble will burst, or if there's a bubble at all. We can only tell after the fact.

So when we see the Bitcoin market only from 2013 to 2014, we see a huge rise in value, just to watch it drop again (there's the bubble bursting). However, if we see Bitcoin's trajectory from 2014 to the present day, we can spot another meteoric rise in value.

Is this a bubble? The answer to that question is way out of the scope of this book. Keep in mind that for physical products (such as a home), there is definitely some inherent value to it. But what about Bitcoin? There is nothing physical that an investor can palpably touch? No, the value of Bitcoin lies in whatever everyone says its worth.

Don't be too afraid though. The same holds true for the $100 bill that only cost 12 cents to make. No rational person would ever trade a $100 bill for twelve cents, even though that's its production value. Rather, the $100 bill is worth exactly that because we all collectively agree that you can buy $100 worth of stuff in exchange for it. The same is true for gold, silver, gems, and yes, Bitcoin.

So if public opinion is what largely drives the value of Bitcoin, what influences public opinion? Specifically, what if Bitcoin begins receiving a whole lot of bad press? What would happen to the value of Bitcoin then?

Interestingly and paradoxically enough, the better a stock is performing, the *more* criticism and negative press it receives! The same rules seem to apply to Bitcoin.

Take a look at what Kerry Close stated publicly in *Time* magazine right after the Bitcoin bubble of 2014: "virtual currency is known for wild fluctuations in price. The value of one Bitcoin—which was created in 2008 by an anonymous programmer or group of programmers—reached its all-time high of $1,165.89 in November 2013 before taking a major dive" (Close 2017).[17] Bad press, no? While Close clearly believed that the value of Bitcoin was going to nosedive, he, along with many other financial investors and analysts, were dead wrong.

Where they were correct is in recognizing Bitcoin's notorious volatility. In the same article, Kerry Close astutely notes that prices "have more or less inched up, and at the turn of the year, they started to approach record highs. On Thursday, the value of a bitcoin reached $1,153.02. However, later Thursday morning, prices suddenly fell by about $200."

---

[17] Information taken from http://time.com/money/4623650/bitcoin-invest/

This sort of volatility, while it does not show up in the graphs above, does occur on a daily basis. For someone to successfully invest in Bitcoin, they must be prepared to receive extraordinary gains, but also know that they may lose a lot of that money overnight.

There is no shortage of this type of bad press for Bitcoin, but does that mean that you should not invest in it? That's something only you can answer based on the amount of risk you're willing to handle in your life– we are simply here to inform you of trends. It is strongly suggested that you seek financial advise before making large investments of any kind.

There is one final and important note in investing in Bitcoin. This cryptocurrency is not the single monolith that many expect. Right after Kerry Close's negative comments on Bitcoin, there was a hidden development in the cryptocurrency world. Perhaps coincidentally, Bitcoin went through what's called a *hard fork* and developed a new cryptocurrency called Bitcoin Cash.

What is Bitcoin Cash?

Just when we thought that Bitcoins would only exist in cyberspace, there comes an oxymoron called **Bitcoin Cash**. Before we delve into what this is, let's first examine the term *hard fork* that led us to this. Remember that when cryptocurrency enthusiasts talk about Bitcoin, they like to throw some of these terms at you. Generally, they are simple terms and *hard fork* is no different.

A **hard fork** *occurs when there is a radical change in the operating protocol of a cryptocurrency rendering a set of transactions valid.* What this means is that Bitcoin is essentially dividing in two and creating another blockchain that would make many transactions valid that otherwise were not so.

This permanent fork in the blockchain suddenly allows streams of income to enter from another group or location. A good way to think of it is like a valve. When you open your sink, you allow water to flow from the pipes and through your faucet. Once you close it, no water is flowing.

The same concept holds true for Bitcoin's blockchain, and because of this, if you think you can suddenly double your money, you're dead wrong. In Bitcoin's hard fork it created another currency called **Bitcoin Cash**.

Bitcoin Cash works exactly like Bitcoin, with its own distributed ledger and miners circulating currency while keeping an eye out for malicious transactions. Also similar to Bitcoin is that it is a P2P compatible currency with no centralized control. So how does it differ from its parent cryptocurrency?

Bitcoin Cash has the potential to be 'scaled.' But what does 'scaling' mean in the cryptocurrency world? Luckily, its definition is the same in business.

Let's work with an example. Imagine that your aunt, Jennifer, is looking to bake some cookies. It takes her an hour to mix the dough, preheat the oven, and bake one cookie. While Jennifer may be full after she eats her one cookie, this isn't the most efficient use of her time and resources.

Soon your aunt decides to buy a larger cookie tray and get the ingredients in bulk. Jennifer soon realizes that while it took her an hour to make one cookie, it takes only slightly more time (say, an hour and five minutes) to bake a dozen cookies. Now she has enough for herself and her family.

But what if Aunt Jennifer wants to make a business out of this? She could invest in a larger oven that can bake a hundred cookies at a time, get better deals is she buys in bulk from providers, and make one hundred cookies per hour. Now she has enough for herself, her family, and to sell. Notice what Jennifer did here. She realized that it took more or less the same amount of time to bake one cookie as it did to bake one hundred cookies.

This is what we mean by scalable. In the cryptocurrency world however, we're not talking one hundred cookies. It must be just as easy to conduct ten transactions, as it is to conduct ten million transactions. This is what Bitcoin Cash brings to the table.

What Is the Difference Between Bitcoin and Bitcoin Cash:

The main difference between Bitcoin Cash and its predecessor is that Bitcoin Cash raises its block size from one megabyte to eight megabytes. This allows for speedier transactions to be conducted along the blockchain. Furthermore, "Bitcoin Cash introduces a new way of signing transactions. This also brings additional benefits such as input value signing for improved hardware wallet security, and elimination of the quadratic hashing problem" (Bitcoin Cash 2017).[18]

Borrowing from the same article, Bitcoin Cash also has wipeout/replay protection. In the case that "two chains persist, Bitcoin Cash minimizes user disruption, and permits safe and peaceful coexistence of the two chains, with well thought out replay and wipeout protection." This hard fork was implemented for many reasons. Some of these reasons, detailed below, will give us further insight into the world of this cryptocurrency.

---

[18] Information taken from https://www.bitcoincash.org

BLOCKCHAIN SCALABILITY:

We have to remember that even though 2008 was not so long ago, it is a lifetime in the cryptocurrency world. When Satoshi first developed Bitcoin, the most advanced processing system at the time allowed for a one-megabyte limit of data per block, which equates to three transactions per second. With the eight-megabyte limit, transactions can be conducted much faster. But so what?

Why did Bitcoin's stock simply skyrocket with the advent of Bitcoin Cash? This doesn't happen when Apple, Microsoft, or Dell create a faster computer. Their stocks stay the same (or perhaps slightly increase over time) with the development of each new technological advance.

Why is Bitcoin so different simply because it can now process transactions at a faster rate? It's important to note that this is the first time Bitcoin has changed its blockchain. While there were many questions as to how this would occur, the fact that Bitcoin simply developed Bitcoin Cash and 'forked' seemed to show investors that it was quite capable and willing to change according to advances in technology; they already knew this about Apple, Microsoft, and Dell.

Second, they noticed that mining has been increasing at a faster and faster pace, yet Bitcoin remained the same. With Bitcoin Cash, investors saw that this cryptocurrency could be enhanced and adapted to advances in Bitcoin mining.

NEW IMPROVEMENTS FOR INCREASED SECURITY:

According to Bitcoin Cash's website, they have singled out new features that are worth noting, including chain scalability (the ability to process many more transactions at once), new transaction signatures, new difficulty adjustment algorithms, and decentralized development.

For new transaction signatures, they adopted a new *SigHash* to provide replay protection, improve wallet security, and eliminate a former quadratic hashing problem. Furthermore, regarding the new difficulty adjustment algorithm, they state that this is a "responsive proof-of-work difficulty adjustment that allows miners to migrate from the legacy Bitcoin chain as desired [To Bitcoin Cash], while providing protection against hashrate fluctuations" (Bitcoin Cash 2017).[19]

DECENTRALIZED DEVELOPMENT:

---

[19] All of the information from this paragraph is taken from https://www.bitcoincash.org/#about

Finally, they had to deal with the problem of decentralized development. Bitcoin Cash notes that with "multiple independent teams of developers providing software implementations, the future is secure. Bitcoin Cash is resistant to political and social attacks on protocol development. No single group or project can control it. The bitcoin-ml (mailing list) is a good venue for making proposals for changes that require coordination across development teams" (ibid.).

WORLD MARKET VALUE OF BITCOIN:

This last point is important, especially for international investors. Unlike the euro, peso, or rupee or others that may be influenced by external forces occurring within the country, Bitcoin Cash is driven by the world market value of its currency. We saw the value of Bitcoin compared to the dollar in the graphs above, but if we were to compare it to the value of the Venezuelan bolivar, we'd be seeing much higher profits for Bitcoin.

This is not because Bitcoin's value has increased. Rather because of strong inflationary practices of the Venezuelan government, their local currency has decreased in value. But if Bitcoin remains the same, or increases in value, what should Venezuelans do? The ones with access to Internet would do well to save their money in Bitcoin rather than in their local currency, which is going to be worth less every single day.

This is all interesting, but how do I get my hands on Bitcoin?

Similar to physical currencies, there is a specific way for someone to save Bitcoin for future transactions. If there is one thing about the world that Bitcoin users know (or should know), it's that one should never over-inundate people with complex information. The world can only allow one change at a time.

BITCOIN WALLETS:

Cryptocurrencies were revolutionary enough, so in order to make people more comfortable with them, they developed **'wallets'** for Bitcoin. These wallets serve the same function and operate in the same way that regular wallets do – they keep your money. There is also an element of anonymity in Bitcoin wallets that we do not have with credit cards and checks. Bitcoin encrypts the user's information, rendering it much more difficult to hack a single user. Below is a simple diagram showing how Bitcoin encrypts personal information so that hackers are left with a tougher time in attempting to steal someone's information.

Figure 6: Example of how Bitcoin Encrypts Information (Source: Bitcoin Core 2017)[20]

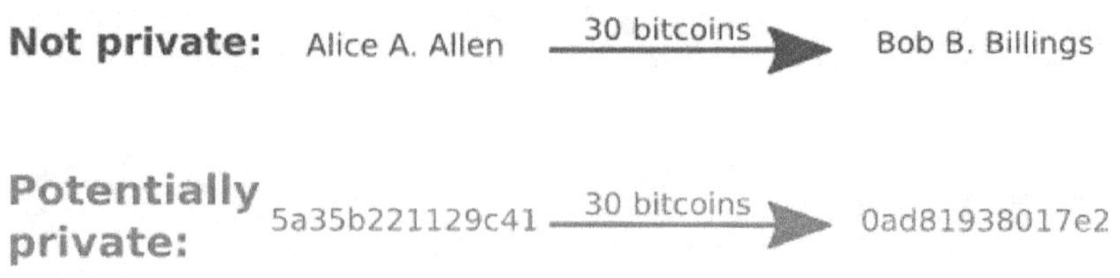

Not private: Alice A. Allen ——30 bitcoins——▶ Bob B. Billings

Potentially private: 5a35b221129c41 ——30 bitcoins——▶ 0ad81938017e2

---

[20] Chart taken from https://bitcoin.org/en/bitcoin-core/features/privacy

USING BITCOIN WALLETS:

Now that we are a bit more comfortable with the potential security benefits of using Bitcoin, let's see how different Bitcoin wallets can be used to buy and sell products online. For the sake of simplicity, we are going to examine each wallet from simplest to most advanced. The average Bitcoin user would be happy with the basic wallets, but in case you're interested in running a business with Bitcoin, we are including some of the more advanced wallet options as well.

There are multiple Bitcoin wallets that you can keep your money in. Without going too in depth into these wallets, let's take a brief look at how they are similar and different from one another. To take a look at these wallets, first visit *https://bitcoin.org/en/getting-started and pick the "Choose Your Wallet" icon. Instead of going in the order shown in their website, we are going to analyze these wallets from simplest to most complex.*

BITCOIN CORE:

First up is Bitcoin Core. This is the easiest and simplest wallet to understand. It offers the high level of security that we have come to associate with distributed ledgers, but none of the bells and whistles that we would see in other wallets. One of the downsides of this wallet is that it occupies a lot of space in your hard drive.

Additionally, according to their website, the security risks exists because "this wallet can be loaded on computers which are vulnerable to malware. Securing your computer, using a strong passphrase, moving most of your funds to cold storage, or enabling two-factor authentication can make it harder to steal your bitcoins" (Bitcoin Core 2017).[21] However, don't be discouraged! All Bitcoin wallets receive the same information on that level.

BITCOIN KNOTS:

The next wallet that we will analyze is **Bitcoin Knots**, which is considered similar to Bitcoin Core. The main difference between Bitcoin Core and Bitcoin Knots is that the latter can hold multiple accounts in the same wallet.

---

[21] Quote taken from
https://bitcoin.org/en/wallets/desktop/windows/bitcoincore/

Let's imagine that John and Mary are married to each other. If they decide to keep their cryptocurrency finances in one place, they can use this wallet. However, should they want to use it for different reasons or decide to split their accounts, they can still log into one account and see different numbers per account, while still using the same wallet.

With Bitcoin Core, this would be impossible as its one wallet per person. As for downsides with Bitcoin Knots, it's the same as with every computer: if your laptop is compromised, there is a great chance that your security information would also be in jeopardy. Both Bitcoin Core and Bitcoin Knots are useful tools for the casual person looking to buy and sell products with Bitcoin. Here are some more advanced wallets that can help you take your business to the next level.

GREEN ADDRESS:

GreenAddress loves to boast its user-friendliness as Bitcoin wallet. Different from *Electrum,* which uses a decentralized server, **GreenAddress** has the classic centralized system. According to the Bitcoin website on GreenAddress, this "wallet is loaded from a remote location.

This means that whenever you use your wallet, you need to trust the developers not to steal or lose your bitcoins in an incident on their site. Using a browser extension or mobile app, if available, can reduce that risk" (Bitcoin 2017).[22]

Because of this centralized security system along with the third party that you Bitcoin involves, GreenAddress is better for personal use rather than business use. I highly suggest that this wallet not be used for any official business transactions, but it should be fine with financial transactions between family and friends.

BITHER:

---

[22] Quote taken from https://bitcoin.org/en/wallets/desktop/windows/greenaddress/

Bither is a relatively simple wallet that could be used by individuals, professionals, or companies. It operates well under iOS, Windows, Android, Mac, and Linux platforms and has a 'cold storage' option. Many Bitcoin wallets tout this feature, so it's worth examining. When someone is operating in 'hot mode,' they are essentially online.

This means that any typical cell phone, once the Bither wallet is downloaded, will be considered *'hot.'* On the other hand, *'cold mode'* is when a computer is offline. Some Bitcoin wallets can allow you to backup information on a 'cold' device—meaning that essentially you have information stored on a computer that is not connected to the Internet. This allows for an extra layer of security for your Bitcoins.

ELECTRUM:

Another relatively simple wallet is **Electrum**, which is famous for its speed and rapidity. Somewhat similar to the blockchain that Bitcoin uses, Electrum's servers are decentralized, which means that there's no lag in the system.

It also offers the hot and cold options that we saw with Bither.

Furthermore, there is an interesting advancement to Electrum that many of the next wallets espouse: **they have two-factor authentication**. Again, this is another cryptocurrency term designed to either confuse you, or leave you with a sense of security.

Here's an easy example: Noelle is accepting Bitcoins from her friends and uses Electrum as her wallet. Just like with any computer login, she needs to present a username and a password. With most websites, this is enough to allow you to enter into their system. However, with two-factor authentication, they would either send Noelle an email, text, or phone call to make sure that she's indeed the person who is attempting to log into her account. This is that 'two-factor' part of the authentication. Most of the next wallets have this system built into their programs.

ARMORY:

Armory is another Bitcoin wallet with many of the features we have seen above. Similar to Bither, Armory allows hot and cold storage to increase safety. For their cold storage option, you "can create your wallet on a computer that never touches the Internet, yet still manage the wallet from an online computer with minimal risk of an attacker stealing your funds" (Armory 2017).[23]

This wallet is clearly meant for businesses, as it would only be a fruitful investment to pay for an offline computer if you know that you're going to be conducting many high-end transactions for your business. On the other hand, if you're simply looking to buy stuff and exchange money in a P2P fashion between friends and family, this wallet seems a bit too advanced for such simple transactions.

ArcBit:

---

[23] Information taken from https://www.bitcoinarmory.com/cold-storage/

The next wallet that we are going to examine is **ArcBit**. This wallet is also featured in the Bitcoin website and has the traditional cold wallet mechanism that we are finding in many storage options.

The main difference between ArcBit and other wallets is that is espouses a remote wallet option. Think of it this way: your wallet is working for you despite the fact that you are not physically next to it. Clearly, this can only work in cyberspace, but that's why it's so effective.

Your wallet is essentially "loaded from a remote location. This means that whenever you use your wallet, you need to trust the developers not to steal or lose your bitcoins in an incident on their site. Using a browser extension or mobile app, if available, can reduce that risk" (Bitcoin 2017).[24]

---

[24] Information taken from https://bitcoin.org/en/wallets/desktop/windows/arcbit/

Similar to other Bitcoin wallets, ArcBit "gives you full control over your Bitcoins. This means no third party can freeze or lose your funds. You are however still responsible for securing and backing up your wallet" (ibid.). According to the Bitcoin website, there is another positive aspect with choosing ArcBit as a wallet.

They state that ArcBit "provides fee suggestions which are based on current network conditions which you can override. This means that this wallet will help you choose the appropriate fee so that your transactions are confirmed in a timely manner without paying more than you have to, but ultimately gives you control if you want to override the suggestion" (ibid.).

BitGo:

The next wallet that we are to evaluate is **BitGo**. This wallet, similar to Armory, is designed for business use, meaning that there are higher levels of security, but at the cost of expediency. It is a multi-sig wallet, meaning that multiple signatures are required to enter into it. Furthermore, it offers the two-factor authorization feature that we have seen in previous wallets.

This wallet also has developed an even more advanced version of itself, *BitGo Instant*. Again, this wallet is best-equipped for large-scale business use, rather than individual or private usage, as its features may be too advanced for the casual transactions between family and friends.

Their website (which seems much more developed than other Bitcoin wallet websites, proudly states that BitGo "allows on-chain, zero confirm, instant transactions between participants. Before BitGo Instant, typical transactions took 10 minutes or more to be recorded in a block by miners" (BitGo 2017).[25]

---

[25] Information taken from https://www.bitgo.com/solutions#wallet

This transaction must then be approved by the miners in Bitcoin, and previously understood as *zero-confirm*. If it weren't for the security features on this wallet, transactions such as these would be treading into dangerous waters because "without BitGo Instant's guarantee, it is possible for the sender to spend the money elsewhere before the transaction is confirmed" (ibid.).

These multiple confirmations would be problematic for the casual user, but not for companies. Furthermore, this solves the potential and proverbial problem of double dipping. The wallet does not allow for someone to spend a Bitcoin on one product and *simultaneously* spend that *same* Bitcoin on another product.

mSIGNA

Finally, the last wallet that we must analyze is **mSIGNA**, another ridiculously complex name for a Bitcoin wallet. Similar to BitGo, their website seems much more advanced than the basic Bitcoin wallets. According to them, mSIGNA is "a next-generation multi-signature wallet. It supports the best security practices in the industry and is rated amongst the most secure wallets by bitcoin.org.

While an advanced tool, it is easy to use. It is very fast, and its inherent scalability offers enterprise-level solutions. And best of all, it's a free and open source" (mSINGA 2017).[26] Other wallets may soon be offering this option, but mSIGNA is the only one that I know of that also offers Litecoin capabilities.

Perhaps there are wallets that are also compatible with Ethereum, Dogecoin, and Ripple, but they do not advertise it much. We will examine the possibilities of other cryptocurrencies in the next question. As for mSIGNA, it also seems much more advanced in its usability and user-friendly account. Below is a snapshot illustrating the difference mSIGNA and Bitcoin Knots.

---

[26] Quote taken from https://ciphrex.com

Figure 7: Differences between mSIGNA and Bitcoin Knots

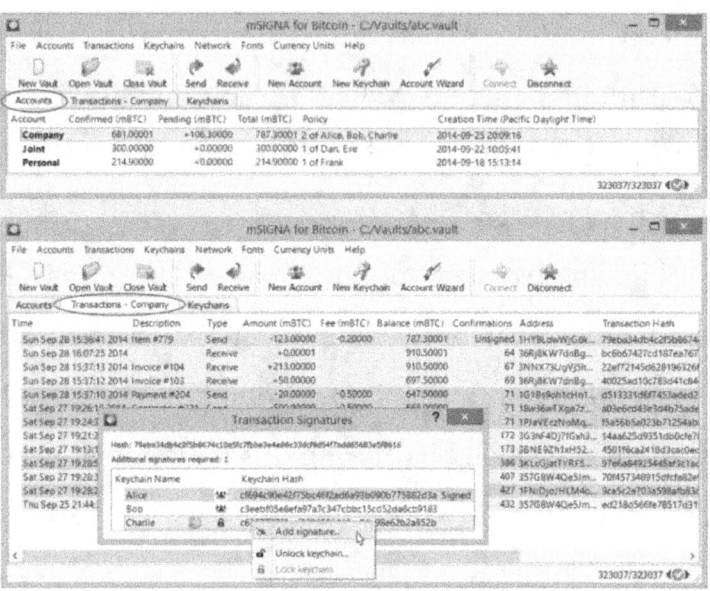

What is Bitcoin Knots?

Bitcoin Knots is a derivative of Bitcoin Core (since 2011 December) with a collection of improvements backported from and sometimes maintained outside of the master git tree. More details on the enhancements in Bitcoin Knots are listed below the downloads.

Please note: Bitcoin Knots includes some new features that have not yet been tested to the same extent as those included in Bitcoin Core. While we make a reasonable effort to ensure they are safe, there are no guarantees. Use of Bitcoin Knots is (as with Bitcoin Core) always at your own risk!

Download Bitcoin Knots

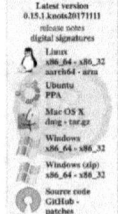

Security notice

Please note: This webserver, like almost all webservers, is not under our exclusive physical access, and therefore cannot be trusted to not be compromised. Always verify the correct PGP signature (from Luke Dashjr's PGP key) on any downloads so avoid risk of malware. Note that his PGP key is also hosted on bitcoin.org, so you can (and should, if you don't already have it from another trusted source) download from at least two independent webservers and ensure they match.

SHA256 hashes of all downloads, signed by Luke Dashjr's PGP key, are available under the "digital signatures" link in the download box. If this link is missing, broken, or fails to verify, do not trust the downloaded files, and contact him immediately.

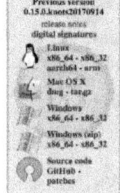

As we can see, while mSIGNA offers an accountant-style wallet with accounts in-and-out, while Bitcoin Knots hasn't seemed to update its profile in a while. That said; don't judge a book by its cover. The most important thing for you to do when choosing a wallet is to make sure that it serves your purposes, despite the graphics.

For complete details on the differences between wallets, I strongly encourage you to visit the Bitcoin wallet website, found at https://bitcoin.org/en/choose-your-wallet. Much of the information here is taken from their website. They also break down the differences in wallets into different tables that allow you to evaluate the pros and cons of each wallet to best pick which option best suits your needs. The next question that we are going to answer is an interesting one, and if you're interested in investing in other cryptocurrencies other than Bitcoin, it is for you.

Are there any other cryptocurrencies other than Bitcoin?

As we have noted time and again, Bitcoin has gained quite a success over the past few years. And, as always in history, whenever there is a stellar success with one industry, many others come in seeking to take advantage of their unprecedented gains. Bitcoin and cryptocurrencies are no different. If you're interested in learning about and investing in cryptocurrencies, then this section is for you. First, while Bitcoin takes the lion's share of crypto-enthusiasm, there is another currency that gives Bitcoin a good run for its money—Ethereum.

ETHEREUM:

Vitalik Buterin, Ethereum's founder, took advantage of the increase in technology from when Bitcoin was first created in 2008 to when Ethereum entered the market in 2013. Because of this, Ethereum espouses a much more advanced blockchain algorithm than its predecessor. And while it competes with Bitcoin as a cryptocurrency, its true claim to fame is elsewhere. Before we analyze the deep differences between Bitcoin and Ethereum, let's see how they both relate as cryptocurrencies.

Just like any cryptocurrency, Ethereum is founded and based upon the blockchain network. In fact, it would be hard to imagine a cryptocurrency that didn't run using blockchain technology. Unlike Bitcoin, whose currency is simply based on supply and demand, with miners creating more and more Bitcoin as we speak, users implementing Ethereum create their own currency, called *ethers*.

These **ethers** are simply units of currency to be employed along the Ethereum blockchain. Bitcoin may be attempting to compete with every government-issue currency (pounds, euros, dollars, yen, yuan, etc.), but Ethereum is sidelining these problems.

According to Coindesk, ethers were not designed to be converted from one currency to another. Rather, they are "meant to pay for specific actions on the Ethereum network, with users receiving it for using their computing power to validate transactions and for contributing to its development" (Coindesk 2017).[27]

Due to it's advanced technology Ethereum is ahead of Bitcoin in its response time. Remember how Bitcoin took 10 minutes to reload? **Ethereum can do the same transaction in 17 seconds!** This means that transactions are essentially 'live' when you're working on them. But how can we apply this to regular life, and how different is it really from Bitcoin?

---

[27] Quote obtained from https://www.coindesk.com/what-to-know-trading-ethereum/

So How is Ethereum (ETH) really Different from Bitcoin?

SMART CONTRACTS:

Ethereum allows the user to create what's called **'smart contracts'** with their platform. A **smart contract** essentially works in the same way a regular contract work, but allows itself to be edited over time. Unlike a paper contract, that would have to be printed out and distributed with every iteration of the contract, a smart contract works a lot like a GoogleDocs document that anyone can edit with changes before they're agreed upon.

Let's imagine a simple scenario: Kathi in New Zealand wants to sell her condo to Terence, living in South Africa. They could physically meet up and agree upon a contract, or pass emails back and forth up until a deal is reached.

However, in order to do this, they would have to go through dozens of middlemen, ranging from realtors, attorneys, insurance companies, and so on. With Ethereum, Kathi just has to create a smart contract that both she and Terence can manipulate. Once they agree upon terms, they can amend the contract as required. Then it's time to sign.

Because smart contracts generate an encrypted code that is unique to any contract, both Kathi and Terence know that they are signing the exact same document. **If even a comma is different, the Ethereum smart contract would generate a completely different encrypted code**, so both parties would be aware that they're signing different contracts. This would be impossible with regular paper and ink. Plus the parties would have to pay for extra individuals to be in the agreement, as lawyers, accountants, and staff would be necessary.

While the example of buying a condo is given here, there could be an almost infinite number of ways that smart contracts, using Ethereum, can revolutionize the way they conduct business. Smart contracts can be used for leases, rental agreements, deeds for next of kin, and so on.

The other way that Ethereum has become revolutionary is that it automates every single aspect of smart contracts. Instead of having humans review documents and line items, computers do the work for them. This allows mortgage companies, financial institutions, and investment firms to save a lot of money on back-end employees that would severely affect their bottom line. This automation also eliminates the possibility of human error, and since the network oversees itself, then security is much tighter than with a centralized database.

Outside of Bitcoin, Ethereum is by far the next cryptocurrency taking a big leap in the stock market. Below is the chart from 2017, where we see Ethereum jump from a few cents to $400 in 2017.

Figure 8: Ethereum Price (2017)

This information, taken from Coindesk, shows how Ethereum has increased in value over the past year. Let's analyze this a bit.

First, as we can see, while the value of Ethereum has really kicked off, there is no comparison between Ethereum's value and Bitcoin's meteoric rise. However, while there are differences in terms of magnitude, their direction is the same—up.

Let's look a bit deeper into the graphs: Sometime in July, Ethereum's value clearly increased at a quick pace. Then from August to September, we saw its value decrease substantially.[28] Take a look at Bitcoin's chart and you will see something similar. Then, with the advent of Bitcoin Cash and Bitcoin's value continuing to skyrocket, Ethereum seems to be riding Bitcoin's coattails.

Investors should always keep in mind that there are many variables influencing the prices of any commodity, but since all cryptocurrencies fall under one specific part of the stock market, they are influenced by many of the same issues.

As you will recall, the main issue that will not influence cryptocurrencies are crises 'on the ground' that would influence fiat currency. If you're interested in investing, I suggest you take a look at Kraken, Coinbase, or Bittrex for platforms on where to invest your cryptocurrencies.

---

[28] For what it's worth, the biggest problem I have with any of the cryptocurrencies right now is people are treating them like they're stocks. They're not stocks. I think that once the amateur traders realize they aren't trading stocks, they'll get out of the market and the bubble will burst.

We are now going to move on to another cryptocurrency—Ripple. However, before we continue, you should know that **there are over 900 cryptocurrencies**, most of which are not worth a penny in the stock market. This means that if you invest small amounts in many of these, you may be able to see some gains. Now let's move on to Ripple.

RIPPLE:

Ripple is an interesting cryptocurrency, and solves an interesting issue. Remember how we were mentioning that it currently takes a bank three to five business days to conduct a simple transaction between friends? This is the issue that Ripple is trying to solve.

Here's the process between banks every time you want to send money over to friends. When you extract money, the bank has to process it, meaning that they must subtract that exact amount from your bank account. This money is then transferred to your friend's bank account; always making sure that it's the exact amount.

Meanwhile, these figures need to be checked by a computer and by employees to ensure that they are identical. Multiply this process out thousands of times and it's really a miracle that they manage to do all of this in three to five business days. But where does Ripple come into play?

As was previously stated, Ripple was created by banks for banks. This means that it was developed as a proxy currency so that trades can occur between financial institutions in seconds and not days.

Let's briefly refer back to the introduction: remember those Chinese merchants who were growing tired of lugging around heavy copper coins around the South China Sea? What they developed was paper money, designed to replace the copper coins while at sea, and then traded for currency when back on land. This allowed the Chinese merchants to carry more cargo and not worry about their currency sinking to the bottom of the ocean if anything happened (they actually had to worry about it flying away from them in a strong wind).

Because they used paper, even if only for sailing at sea, they were able to gain a competitive advantage over other merchants. Ripple is essentially offering the 21st century version of this for banks. They have a proxy currency for P2P transactions between friends, families, and institutions. This is another form of what is called **FinTech**.

FinTech:

FinTech, or financial technology, is another term loved by cryptocurrency users. Financial technology can mean almost anything, but its most important quality is that it makes conducting transactions between individuals, institutions, and banks easier and more efficient.

The Chinese merchants collectively deciding to use paper instead of copper coins is a rudimentary example of FinTech.

Ripple offers this sort of service, and its goal "is to enable people to break free from the 'walled gardens' of financial networks – i.e., credit cards, banks, PayPal and other institutions that restrict access with fees, charges for currency exchanges and processing delays" (Coindesk 2013).[29] Tearing down these 'walled gardens' is another form of advancing speeds and performance of currencies, which is what FinTech is all about.

The other main difference between Ripple, Ethereum, and Bitcoin is how these currencies are produced: While Bitcoin involves mining and you can create your own currency with Ethereum (ethers), Ripple takes a very small sum of money per transaction and puts it into the network. This is how it is reproduced, and it's quite an insignificant sum.

---

[29] Information taken from **https://www.coindesk.com/10-things-you-need-to-know-about-ripple/**

Furthermore, the "amount is destroyed rather than retained. The deduction is meant as to safeguard against the system being swamped by any one individual who might try to put through millions of transactions at once" (Coindesk 2013). Additionally, because all of the Ripple in the world already exists (it is a pre-mined cryptocurrency, as if this couldn't get any weirder), there is no way to create currency.

Instead, they burn off a bit from each transaction, which works in exactly the opposite way than every other currency! You're still creating demand, but instead of starting with zero and increasing supply, you're now starting off with 100 billion Ripples, and lowering the number from there onward. With Ripple, you're burning cash and making money at the same time!

LITECOIN:

Let's now look at what seems to be Bitcoin 2.0—Litecoin. Admittedly, there is little to get excited about regarding Litecoin as it's so similar to its predecessor, who is, by the way, much more famous and valuable. However, there are plenty of similarities between these two coins that it's worth mentioning Litecoin as a potential supplement to Bitcoin. Let's see how the differences play out:

First of all, you can get your Litecoin at https://litecoin.org. Similar to Bitcoin, it's primarily a P2P interface adopting blockchain technology and working as a cryptocurrency. If you go to their website, you'll find that Litecoin "enables instant, near-zero cost payments to anyone in the world. Litecoin is an open source, global payment network that is fully decentralized without any central authorities. Mathematics secures the network and empowers individuals to control their own finances. Litecoin features faster transaction confirmation times and improved storage efficiency than the leading math-based currency" (Litecoin 2017).[30] The decentralized aspect of Litecoin, along with the 'math-based currency' that they are touting is quite similar to Bitcoin.

What's the Difference Between Bitcoin and Litecoin?

One of the main differences between Bitcoin and Litecoin is that while Bitcoin uses SHA-256 (along with most other cryptocurrencies) as its coding language, Litecoin implements another language, called *Scrypt*. While for investors, there is hardly a difference (or importance) in the coding language that these cryptocurrencies use there are some back-end differences worth noting that may influence investment.

---

[30] Quote taken from https://litecoin.org

It is generally agreed upon that Scrypt is an extremely safe computer coding language. While its safety may be more pronounced than SHA-256, there is little evidence that SHA-256 has ever been unsafe. Here's the other part of the story: SHA-256 has been tested out 'in the world' so to speak, and because of this, we have more evidence that it is a successful program for computer coding.

Scrypt, on the other hand, due to its relative newness, remains an unknown quantity. It's arguably safer than SHA-256, but hasn't had the public testing that SHA-256 has gone through.

The second difference between Bitcoin and Litecoin is the number of Litecoins in existence. As opposed to Ripple, which is already pre-mined, and Ethereum's 'create your own currency' policy, Litecoin and Bitcoin's coins must be mined.

You will recall that Bitcoin had 21 million coins as its cap. No more Bitcoins were ever to be mined, but if demand continued to increase, there would be a halving of each Bitcoin (not its value, just number). This could continue *ad infinitum*. Litecoin has announced that there will be 84 million Litecoin in existence; exactly four times as many Bitcoin.

But why is this the case? Well, Litecoin was developed a few years after Bitcoin, using pretty much the same formula but with better technology. Because of this, the time it takes to create a Litecoin is exactly four times as fast as with Bitcoin. Whereas the average Bitcoin miner had to wait the usual ten minutes for the block to be completed, with Litecoin, this can be done in two and a half minutes.

However, there is no comparison between Litecoin and Ethereum's seventeen-second lag. Because of this faster Litecoin reproduction, developers can engage in even quicker transaction times. Miners in Litecoin's world are rewarded with twenty-five Litecoins for every block in the blockchain network.

Similar to Bitcoin, the extant Litecoins gets halved every 4 years (sound familiar? Just like Bitcoin). This means that for every 840,000 blocks, the Litecoins get halved. Predictably, Litecoin uses the same formula as Bitcoin, leaving us with 84 million Litecoin.

There clearly are some differences between Bitcoin and Litecoin, but because they are so similar, the gain of one may be the demise of the other. This would not be the case with Ethereum and Ripple, which are completely different and seek to solve completely separate problems, smart contracts and bank-to-bank transfers, respectively.

While there is no denying that Litecoin is a faster, more reliable, currency than Bitcoin, is it perhaps too similar to its predecessor? Investors should feel comfortable in investing in Litecoin after witnessing the success of Bitcoin, but the million-dollar question is whether or not there will be a market for Litecoin given Bitcoin's unprecedented success.

Will Bitcoin completely replace fiat currency (regular money)?

This is a speculative question to be sure, but let's give it a shot. First things first—only time will tell if Bitcoin (or any other cryptocurrency) will replace fiat currency (regular money). We will first examine arguments for why it may well replace physical cash, and then we will examine arguments for why it will not.

ARGUMENTS FOR THE REPLACEMENT OF FIAT CURRENCY WITH CRYPTOCURRENCY:

Money is simply a tool by which we buy and sell our products. As we have seen throughout the course of this book, money itself has little or no value. What matters is what money represents. As proof of this, it costs the United States Mint 12 cents to make a $100 bill. Clearly the production cost of the bill was only 12 cents, but its value is so much more. However, we are encountering some very real problems with physical currency.

For example, it costs more money to make a penny than the penny is worth. This may still be a bit of a joke, but what happens when this is the case for the nickel, dime, quarter, and dollar? Bitcoin has the potential to replace physical currency *production values.*

What does this mean? Because Bitcoin mining uses up no natural resources (as opposed to mining for gold, copper, or silver, or printing on paper with ink), its production cost is essentially zero. In the future, and with a more technologically advanced world where money will be transferred between machines, and not from hand to hand, it will make a lot of sense to incorporate some type of cryptocurrency to handle these scenarios. Bitcoin is currently best poised to be this currency.

The second reason that Bitcoin will replace fiat money is that its value is not contingent upon world events. The Venezuelan bolivar is going down the drain? No problem. Mugabe in Zimbabwe wants to print more and more money? No worries! Bitcoin is relatively immune to these national policies because it is a worldwide currency.

Because the value of Bitcoin is spread collectively all over the world, what happens in one small country does not affect the value of Bitcoin much. However, if there's a systemic problem with Bitcoin that touches every corner of the world, then we will see investors running away from this cryptocurrency.

However, up until then, because Bitcoin transcends borders, there is a great incentive to use this currency to hedge against fiat currency is the local country. While this may not replace physical money worldwide, there would be a large contingent happy to keep their savings inflation free in Bitcoin, rather than seeing it wasted away in their local currency.

The final reason why Bitcoin may replace fiat currency is that **it seems to be the next level of the ascent of money.**

What do I mean by this? As we have seen, money once did not exist—we traded bushels of wheat for barrels of water. The transactions were slow and unique. This system of barter worked for a while, but soon we developed coins to represent a certain amount of money. These coins later were replaced with paper, and later with credit cards.

It seems like the next step in the evolution of money is for paper currency to be replaced with some type of cryptocurrency. Whether this means that it will be Bitcoin still remains to be seen, but the trajectory of money certainly is pointing in this direction.

ARGUMENTS WHY CRYPTOCURRENCY WILL NOT REPLACE FIAT CURRENCY:

There are also a few reasons as to why many believe Bitcoin will not replace fiat currency:

First in the list are banks and governments. These are the two institutions that will lose if Bitcoin, or any other cryptocurrency begins to compete with them, and they may put up a good fight to stop the rise of cryptocurrencies. Governments uniting together to halt the progress of Bitcoin because pounds, rials, dinars, and bolivars are losing remain a real enough possibility. That said, it hasn't happened yet, but it's something to keep in the back of your mind if you're investing in this cryptocurrency.

Second, it takes just one instance of somebody using Bitcoin or another cryptocurrency to pay for drugs or any type of illicit behavior for the government to step in and create a reason for eliminating the cryptocurrency.

To attract the united ire and wrath of the United States Congress is not something cryptocurrencies should hope to do, especially if members from both parties are unhappy with the direction of Bitcoin. Cases such as these may allow dollars, euros, and rubles to remain in circulation much longer than we may anticipate.

This scenario would lengthen even further if bank workers, currency exchange workers, airport services, and financial accountants decide to unionize against the prevailing cryptocurrency winds. They may hold off the transformation of money from fiat currency to cryptocurrency because their jobs and careers are at stake.

CONCLUSION: IS IT TOO LATE TO GET INVOLVED?

It is never too late to get involved in Bitcoin investments. However, cryptocurrency investors must keep a few things in mind when investing in Bitcoin:

First: this is quite possibly the most erratic investment you will undertake. Over the few weeks that it took to create an outline for this book, Bitcoin's value jumped from $9000 to $17,000, just to plummet another $3,000 in fewer than four hours. Imagine for a moment losing $3,000 in four hours? You probably wouldn't be too happy.

According to Jethro Mullen from CNN Money, "trading has become especially frenzied in recent weeks as new investors have dived into the volatile market. Before Friday's fall, it had gained roughly $5,000 in the previous 48 hours (Mullen 2017)."[31] A high threshold for losing money is necessary for investing in Bitcoin, not only in its official value, but also in the platform you use, as there are many scams out there.

Mullen expands, stating that some "have gone bust altogether and others have suffered cyber heists in which hackers have made off with huge sums. The latest example is digital currency site NiceHash, where bitcoins worth more than $70 million were stolen this week" (Mullen 2017).

But what does Wall Street make of this? It appears that one of the largest drivers of Bitcoin's growth is that many Fortune 500 companies are looking to incorporate blockchain technology into their portfolios and long-term investments. Nonetheless, big banks "who have a complicated relationship with digital currencies – have issued a warning about the dangers of Bitcoin's future, saying the risks haven't been properly studied" (Ibid.). If banks unite to create a different cryptocurrency outside of Bitcoin, yet adopting blockchain technology, it may be a blow to Bitcoin's value.

---

[31] Quote taken from http://money.cnn.com/2017/12/08/investing/bitcoin-latest-price/index.html

Another attack on Bitcoin is coming from an unusual, yet growing, angle: environmentalists. Unlike physical currencies, Bitcoin isn't tied to any central bank. Instead, they are mined by computers with ASIC chips in "vast data centers that guzzle huge amounts of energy.

Bitcoin uses about 32 terawatts of energy every year (enough to power about three million U.S. households). […] By comparison, processing the billions of Visa transactions that take place each year consumes the same amount of power as just 50,000 American homes" (Shane 2017).[32] As we can see, attacks against Bitcoin have been coming from various angles, yet Bitcoin is still rising…

---

[32] Information taken from http://money.cnn.com/2017/12/07/technology/bitcoin-energy-environment/index.html?iid=EL

How do you get started?

Now that we got the bad news out of the way, let's make space for the good news. Here are some platforms and exchanges where you can buy and sell cryptocurrencies (especially Bitcoin) on the world market: **Coinbase, Kraken, and Bittrex**. There may be others, but you have to remain very wary of their ethical practices, as reports of scamming abound.

These three platforms seem to be much more legitimate than some of their counterparts. Investing in Bitcoin is inherently risky business due to the erratic nature of its value—the last thing you want is to worry about the integrity of the platform you're trading on. As always, speak to your financial advisor before investing in any cryptocurrency; we're only here to give you the most important information.

Bitcoin has grown tremendously over the past year—and this is just the beginning. While the value of Bitcoin is high (over $10,000), you don't need this much capital to invest. With the wallets and trading platforms named in this work, you can invest in a fraction of a Bitcoin stock.

Generally there is a limit to how little money you can invest, but these figures range in the tens or hundreds of dollars, not ten thousand. This means that the initial investor of Bitcoin could start off with investing only a twentieth of the a single bitcoin ($500) and potentially see it grow. More and more people are getting excited about the promises of Bitcoin and the future of blockchain technology. With more enthusiasm comes higher values for cryptocurrencies, and Bitcoin, being no different plays by the same rules of the market.

Looking to the Future:

The future of Bitcoin and cryptocurrencies does look bright indeed. Clearly, Bitcoin has taken the lion's share of public scrutiny because of its amazing run in 2017, but the future of cryptocurrencies (including Ethereum, Ripple, and even Litecoin) looks quite promising.

As you can gather from the last few questions we answered above, we still don't know if Bitcoin is an anomaly in the cryptocurrency world or if it is here to stay. There are many uncertainties with Bitcoin, but **the one aspect of Bitcoin that seems to be more permanent and transferable to other industries is the use of blockchain technology.** This technology allows for linkages between many different industries that may begin to invest in it.

Bitcoin is the first currency to adopt blockchain technology as a tool for its operation. The benefits of blockchain technology permeate into banks, financial institutions, governments, and individuals. They may be able to adopt this technology in a relatively stable and hack-free manner.

As with any technology, it can be used for good and bad reasons. Bitcoin is no different. At the risk of sounding cliché, the future of Bitcoin is largely in the hands of those who decide to use it, meaning that it could be you.

GLOSSARY

ArcBit: a Bitcoin-based wallet where you could store your money.

Armory: a Bitcoin-based wallet used mainly for large institutions where you could store your money in cold or hot modes.

ASIC chips: application-specific integrated circuit chips used to mine Bitcoin.

Barter: original system of exchanging goods and services without mediums of exchange (money).

Bitcoin Cash: appearing from a hard fork in Bitcoin's blockchain; operating as a similar P2P and decentralized blockchain network without the oversight of a third party or centralized government.

Bitcoin Core: the original Bitcoin-based wallet; simplest and the wallet with the least amount of features.

Bitcoin Knots: the second iteration of Bitcoin-based wallets where you could store your money; more advanced than Bitcoin Core.

Bitcoin: first worldwide cryptocurrency adopting blockchain technology and capable of conducting payments in a digital fashion.

BitGo: a Bitcoin-based wallet used mainly for large institutions where you could store your money in cold or hot modes; allows for two-factor authentication.

Bither: a standard Bitcoin-based wallet where you could store your money; mostly for individual purposes.

Bittrex: a platform on which to trade Bitcoin and other cryptocurrencies.

Blocks: the foundational elements of blockchain technology; each block consists of a nonce, timestamp, root hash, and previous hash; all blocks are attached to each other through a chain.

Centralized ledger: original system of saving documents where all inputs and fiscal transactions are recorded into one supercomputer storing and maintaining all of the digital information of the network in one location.

Chains: the links binding blocks in the blockchain together; relatively simple concepts compared to the block itself.

Coinbase: a platform on which to trade Bitcoin and other cryptocurrencies.

Cryptocurrency: any non-physical Internet-based currency; derived from the Greek word hidden (meaning *crypt-*) currencies, or mediums of exchange, incorporating complicated algorithms to encrypt data on a blockchain network; defining features of cryptocurrencies are their lack of palpability along with their adoption of blockchain technology.

Decentralized ledger: a middle ground between centralized ledgers and distributed ledgers, where supercomputers act as nodes for smaller networks of computers in a much larger network; considered safer than a centralized ledger, but not as safe as a distributed ledger.

Distributed ledger: a unique system that records documents onto every network account; implemented by every cryptocurrency using blockchain technology.

Electrum: a Bitcoin-based wallet where you could store your money.

Ether: the cryptocurrency developed by Ethereum to conduct transactions on a blockchain network.

Ethereum: a blockchain-based cryptocurrency that creates ethers as its currency; creates smart contracts for customers.

Fiat Currency: paper money currency in circulation and backed by the full force of the government.

FinTech: an abbreviated term for 'financial technology;' oftentimes considered as an approach rather than a system of governing currency exchanges.

GreenAddress: a Bitcoin-based wallet where you could store your money.

Hard Fork: a radical and complete alteration in protocols of cryptocurrencies rendering another set of transactions valid, similar to a valve on a faucet.

Kraken: a platform on which to trade Bitcoin and other cryptocurrencies.

Litecoin: a cryptocurrency extremely similar to Bitcoin, yet with 84 million coins instead of the 21 million that Bitcoin would use; Scrypt computer coding language instead of SHA-256.

Mining: the electronic process by which Bitcoin is created; some cryptocurrencies do not allow mining (e.g., Ripple is pre-mined).

mSIGNA: a Bitcoin-based wallet where you could store your money.

Nonce: a random series of digits whose field value is fixed and unalterable so the hash complies with rules within the blockchain network; generally considered the zeros before a number.

Previous hash: the encrypted code, similar to the root hash, yet incorporating all of the codes from previous blocks; this hash indicates where the block originated.

Ripple: a cryptocurrency developed to facilitate interactions among financial institutions and eliminating needs for human interaction with currencies.

Root hash: a hash acting as proof that certain blocks were created; works as the identification of each block; goes by pseudonyms such as Merkle hash and Merkle root.

Scaling: the process by which a company can create 10 units of a product, and 10,000 units, with the same ease.

Scrypt: developed after SHA-256 and is considered the computer language for Litecoin.

SHA-256: computer language adopted by Bitcoin and other cryptocurrencies.

Smart contract: 21st century contract allowing for exchanges in property, money and financial investments in a 'live' fashion that does not need human interference or supervision; considered smart because it learns from itself.

Timestamp: perhaps the simplest part of the block in blockchain technology indicating when the block was created; timestamps cannot be altered or removed, creating another level of security for cryptocurrency users

Wallet: a place to store your cryptocurrency; purposefully simple term for what they really do.

About the Author

Phillip Westbrook is a seasoned investor, venture capitalist and adjunct professor. An early commentator on bitcoin, his theories and analyses have gained wide respect and deference in the financial world. Due to his many profitable investments, Phillip retired at age 43 and now spends his time teaching, advising, writing and enjoying his wife and 3 daughters. He and his family divide their time between their home in Providence, RI and their summer home in his wife's hometown of Cinque Terre, Italy.